John & Betty Stam: A Story of Triumph

John and Betty Stam:
A Story of Triumph

by

Mrs. Howard Taylor
An Overseas Missionary Fellowship Book

MOODY PRESS
CHICAGO

© 1935 by
THE CHINA INLAND MISSION
PHILADELPHIA
Moody Press Revised Edition, 1982

Former Title: *The Triumph of John and Betty Stam*

Library of Congress Cataloging in Publication Data

Taylor, Howard, Mrs.
  John and Betty Stam: a story of triumph

  Rev. ed. of: The triumph of John and Betty Stam. 1949.
  "An Overseas Missionary Fellowship book."
  1. Stam, John Cornelius, 1907-1934. 2. Stam, Elisabeth
Alden Scott, 1906-1934. 3. Missionaries—China—Bi-
ography. 4. Missionaries—United States—Biography. I.
Title.
BV3427.S8T3   1982   266'.0092'2 [B]   81-22523
ISBN 0-8024-8849-8   AACR2

2 3 4 5 6 7 Printing/LC/Year 87 86 85 84 83

Printed in the United States of America

To the
young people of all lands
before whom lies
the great opportunity of
today and tomorrow

Contents

FOREWORD

THIS BRIEF RECORD is not a eulogy; it is a simple narration of facts. Nothing can be more eloquent than such facts. We do not need to be told that it is day when the sun is shining. Over the portal of the greatest gallery of heroes the world has ever seen stands the brief but divine commendation: "Of whom the world was not worthy."

There are few who feel the loss of John and Betty Stam more deeply than the members of the mission to which they belonged. Such faith and love and devotion are the richest treasures we possess, next only to the harvest of precious souls that God is giving. These dear names are added to a lengthening martyr roll. Think what that means of wealth, over there, where God Himself is seen as "the Lamb that hath been slain." He died to redeem; they died in making known, at His command, that glorious redeeming work. And still He is seeking those who will live —and die, if need be —that He may "see of the travail of his soul and be satisfied." To all eternity we shall live and reign with Christ, but shall we ever be able to make sacrifices for Him again? When sin and pain and death are no more, and all tears are wiped away, shall we ever have again the privilege that is ours now of sharing the fellowship of His sufferings "to seek and to save that which was lost"?

The smile that lingered on the face of John Stam, long after he fell on that Chinese hillside, surely makes for us a rift into the eternal glory. The sweetness of that little baby, loved by the world, surely tells us of the tenderness with which the Lord accepted the "spikenard very precious" of the mother's outpoured life, and of the love with which she is comforted forever and forever. Ours is the opportunity today.

O God, to us may grace be given,
To follow in their train.

M.G.T.

237 West School Lane
Philadelphia

O that it were as it was wont to be,
When Thy old friends of fire, all full of Thee,
Fought against frowns with smiles; gave glorious chase
To persecutions; and against the face
Of Death and fiercest dangers, durst with brave
And sober pace, march on to meet a Grave.

Little, alas, thought they
Who tore the fair breasts of Thy friends,
Their fury but made way
For Thee, and served them in Thy glorious ends.

What did their weapons but set wide the doors
For Thee? fair, purple doors, of Love's devising.
It was the wit of Love o'erflow'd the bounds
Of Wrath, and made Thee way through all those wounds.

RICHARD CRASHAW, 1616-1649

"We are finding that our big problems
are little to His power and that our
little things are great to His love."

JACOB STAM, LL.B

12

1

A Holland Home

IN THE OLDER PART of the city of Paterson, New Jersey, stands the simple frame house built by Peter Stam for his growing family. Reached by a steep flight of steps from the street, it is the highest building of Temple Hill, the cupola above the attic affording extensive views of the city and its surroundings, the nearer hills, the valley of the Hudson, and the wonderful skyline of New York.

When John Stam, the fifth of six tall sons, was growing up, the home overflowed with boys and girls as well as music. English was the language spoken, though there were frequent lapses into the familiar, well-loved Holland tongue, for the parents had come from that brave little country, and their character and traditions savored of its sterling qualities.

Two great blessings had come to Peter Stam on his arrival to the states seeking his fortune. First and best, he had found Christ. A friendly woman had given him a New Testament printed in the two languages, Holland and English, praying that it might speak to his heart. Keen to learn English, he studied it eagerly; it was just what he needed. But before long he forgot his quest for

English in the far deeper quest for salvation. For Peter Stam came to see himself in the light of God.

The Book told me that I was a sinner. Of course, my proud nature rebelled. It told me I was lost. I tried not to believe it; but as I read on I had to be honest with myself, and confess that I was indeed a sinner. My life had been lived entirely to self. . . .

But the Book told me that God loved me; that He "so loved the world [and that meant me], that he gave his only begotten Son, that whosoever believeth in him should not perish [that too meant me], but have everlasting life."

Then and there I closed with the offer. I believed the Word of God, and received Christ as my own personal Saviour. I surrendered my life to Him who died for me, and began by His grace to live for others, because the love of Christ constrained me.

That living for others had resulted, by the blessing of God, in a ministry that had widened with the years until Peter Stam was the loving-hearted "servant of all men" in Paterson for Christ's sake. In the jail, in the hospitals and alms houses, in the poorest sections of the city, in saloons, and on the streets his tall figure and kindly face were familiar to Paterson people. Receiving no salary for his work of love, he developed at the same time his business as a contractor. Many were the houses he put up in the suburbs of the growing city, and so thorough was the workmanship that there was rarely a complaint from the occupants. The business increased until it included real estate, insurance, and a lumber yard, the latter affording endless delight to his own youngsters on Temple Hill.

For the second great blessing that had come to Peter Stam in his adopted country was the brave little Holland girl who became his wife. He had met her in Paterson, and there their home had been established on God-fearing lines. Partly French-Huguenot by descent, she had a deeply religious nature and had early come to know Christ as her Savior and Friend. So the young couple were one in all their aspirations, and the home was a home of love that deepened with the years. Six sons were born to them and three daughters, one of whom died in infancy. John was the seventh in the family, having a younger brother and sister.

Near Temple Hill was the Christian grammar school which the children attended, with its decidedly helpful influence, but the most important part of their education was carried on at home. For Mr. and Mrs. Stam, in a very practical way, gave the first place in their family life to the things of God. Three times every day, when the table was set for meals, Bibles were placed ready, one for each person. Before the food was served, prayer was offered, and then a chapter was read, each person taking part. That still happens in the Stam household three times every day. It is a benediction to be present at the family meals, so real and reverent is the consciousness of the unseen presence. In that way, the Bible took first place in the daily intercourse of parents and children. It was the foundation, the common meeting-ground, the test and arbiter of all their thinking. It held and satisfied their hearts.

Next to that was the love of books and music, which bound the family together.

"We certainly were brought up on books," is the remembrance of the older sister, "and we all had to take music lessons. Father spared no expense to give us the best in these ways. And how we did enjoy our family orchestra!"

Those musical evenings were a great feature in the home life, and did not a little to keep the young people from worldly influences. Discipline was well maintained wherever Mr. Stam was in control. His authority was unquestioned, and though intensely loving he was staunch on matters of conviction. No child of his should be able to say about such things as smoking, theater-going, and dancing, "Father thought it was all right." But although both parents were agreed as to the stand they took, they did their best to make up for disappointments. A trip to New York, a day at the shore, a good concert, or some new instrument for their orchestra would give more lasting pleasure, as the young people discovered, than the excitement of the movies. And then the parents were prepared to deny themselves. They had no radio in their home, for example, pleasant though it would have been in some ways. But, as Mr. Stam said:

> We had seen too much of children drinking in what, to them, is poison! Their souls were worth more to us than the whole world. All our children loved the Word of God. There was never any complaint about the Bible being read at table before every meal. We talked with them, explained our position, and prayed with them. And we sought grace to live consistently. You are so often in your own way, when you undertake to rear children!

Meanwhile, the evangelistic work in which Mr. Stam and the whole family were engaged was growing, like the business. Love wins its way, and from little beginnings down on River Street the work had developed into what is now known as the Star of Hope Mission. Its present spacious home was a disused livery stable when Mr. Stam first found it, festooned with cobwebs and alive with rats. It occupied a fine position, however, in the heart of the city, and was successfully transformed into a good auditorium, seating six hundred,

16

with room for all the other accommodation needed. People of many nationalities are being reached through the Star of Hope Mission. Hundreds have been led to Christ by its workers in the open air, in cottage meetings and house-to-house visitation, as well as in prisons, hospitals, and asylums. Scores of young people, converted and trained in the mission, have gone on to other fields, at home and abroad, and still the Word of God is being sent out from the old center in no fewer than forty languages.

"Ebenezer" is the motto of the family and mission, "Hitherto hath the Lord helped us," but as Mr. Stam loves to testify, to them it means, "Hitherto hath the Lord done it all."

It might have been expected, under such influences, that John would develop early into the Christian life. His brothers and sisters were all truly converted and became workers in the mission. But John had troubles all his own. Doubtless they all had, but his took longer to overcome. He was just an ordinary boy, bright and independent by nature and eager to be helpful. Even as a little fellow he would sew on a button for himself rather than leave it to Mother, and later on, if a garden path had to be laid or a tree rooted up, he was the one to pitch in and do it. At school, though not brilliant in his work, he is remembered for his unusual courtesy and faithfulness in little things. His father would have helped him to continue his studies, but John did not at that time care about higher education. He wanted to go into business, and when he was graduated from the Christian grammar school he took up bookkeeping and stenography. He attended a business college for two years, and at fifteen was so tall and manly that he looked more like twenty.

Inwardly they were difficult years. It was a restless,

upset period in his life. Later on, he developed business ability and was prompt and orderly. But for the time being, things did not go well, and the boy was a puzzle to himself and others. He did not realize that the trouble was that he was trying to live his own life, apart from the grace and help of God. At the Star of Hope he was accustomed to seeing the wonderful transformations that take place when hearts are opened to receive Christ in all His saving power. But he, John Stam, was not like the drunkards, down-and-outs, and people ignorant of the gospel who were saved at the mission. From a child he had known it all, and, in a sense, believed it all. Yet he was in the "far country" just as truly as the prodigal of old, and all the more in danger because of his self-righteousness.

Conversion has been defined as the process, gradual or sudden, by which a self-hitherto divided, consciously wrong and unhappy, becomes unified, consciously right and happy, through its acceptance of divine realities. And that was just the change that took place, by the mercy of God, when John Stam "came to himself" and came to his Father. Never could he forget the profound conviction of sin that overwhelmed him when, as a lad of fifteen, he was awakened under the preaching of a blind evangelist who was conducting special services at the mission. There, in the familiar surroundings, but in an altogether new way, he saw himself as lost and helpless apart from Christ. Hell became real to him as never before—the awful end of a Christless life. No one who has not experienced it can imagine what such conviction of sin means, when the soul seems to stand already at the bar of judgment, in the pure light of God. That was the experience that changed John Stam from the restless, unsatisfied boy he had been to the steadfast man of God that he became.

It was in the classroom of the business school, seated at his desk, that he definitely handed over his life to the Lord. It was a spring day in 1922, and from that time John knew that he was not his own and rejoiced more and more to be at the service of his Master. He still went on with his business training, and in the next six years held office positions in Paterson and New York. But his ambition to make money and get on in life was not what it had been. His chief interest was steadily shifting toward the things of God.

At first when he surrendered to Christ, self-consciousness kept him from taking an open stand. He had a special dread of being called upon to speak in a street meetings, and would go a long way around to avoid a group singing or preaching in the open air. It was a challenge from his father that threw him back on God. Summer had come, and the open-air work was not yet begun. Inwardly concerned, John asked why the band was not out preaching.

"It's up to you, John, to make a beginning," was the unexpected reply.

"That staggered me," he wrote not long after, "but I went ahead. I had to! God blessed those first half-hearted efforts, taking away the fear that old school friends might see me and smile, and filling my heart with joy and blessing."

So fearless did he become in this work that, with his younger brother, Neal, he was out almost every summer evening witnessing for Christ on some street corner. A whole new man, unified, consciously right and happy in the Lord —it was a great change and it affected every part of life.

For John woke up after his conversion intellectually as well as spiritually. He became a great reader, a new love of the beautiful sprang into being, and self-absorption gave place to a lively interest in others. Commuting every day to New York, he would spend a couple of hours in study. He used to travel with three other young men, one of whom was a good Greek scholar, and by sitting together in the cars and ferry they could have a regular Greek lesson. And how New York enlarged his vision! From his office windows overlooking Battery Park, he could watch the shipping of all nations coming and going, where ocean freight and tourist paths converge from everywhere. He once walked the whole length of Manhattan Island, and often explored not only Broadway and Fifth Avenue, with their dazzling display of wealth, but the Ghetto, Chinatown, Pushcart Lane, Greenwich Village, and other quarters frequented by foreigners and artists. It was human nature he loved to study, even more than museums and books.

And the outcome of it all was that a call sounded ever more clearly in his heart to give his whole time directly to soul-saving work. Resigning his business position against the almost indignant remonstrance of his employer, he spent some months helping in the Star of Hope Mission and then went to Chicago for further study and training at Moody Bible Institute. And there was something unusual about that step that was characteristic of the man.

2

Chicago and Proving God

I‍T WAS NOT only for further study in view of his lifework that John Stam went to Moody Bible Institute. He had another purpose in view that was just as important. He realized his need of faith to be even greater than his need of knowledge —faith based upon a personal experience of the faithfulness of God. Up to that time he had never been cast upon God alone for the supply of temporal needs. He had always had a good home and had been earning a sufficient salary to enable him to lay by a little. But now he was committed to missionary work, at home or abroad, and might have to go forward in faith, trusting God alone for supplies. He might be in a position where the help of man would fail or be inadequate. Could he, literally, bank upon the promises of God? Theoretically, he believed that "God's work, done in God's way, will never lack God's supplies," but would it work out practically? That was the question to which he must find an answer in personal experience.

Going to Chicago supplied an opportunity for testing both himself and the promises of Scripture. His family understood that he had saved up enough to pay his way for a year or two at the Institute, and they took it for granted that he would let his needs be known, later on, as they might arise. That John decided not to do. He would get work in Chicago, if the Lord were pleased to provide for him in that way, or he would accept help that might be given in answer to prayer. His needs should be known to God alone. And in his heart the voice was heard: "Act as if I were, and you shall find that I am."

It was a plunge into a new life indeed, when John found himself one of a thousand students at the Moody Bible Institute.

Everything goes like clockwork around Moody's [wrote one of his brothers who called to see him]. It has to, with such a crowd! And everything is early — breakfast at 7, lunch at 12:30, supper at 5:30, and meals are through in half an hour. Practically every student does some work . . . and in such a happy spirit! Hymn singing bursts out all over the place, kitchens and washrooms included, all the time.

It goes like clockwork [wrote another visitor], but the spirit in the wheels is intensely genial. How Wesley would have blessed such work and commended it! The confraternity of the workers is most inspiring. They are so varied, but all have a common purpose. Everywhere one feels that Jesus is in the midst and that the Bible is honored.

If the buildings were old and the facilities rather meager, as John discovered, the curriculum was not meager. It was surprisingly full and thoroughgoing. John entered the missionary course at first, which included many practical subjects, but was transferred to the general (Bible) course a year later. He made very good grades, obtaining high marks in all his chief subjects and impressing his teachers as "a young man of

22

arresting personality and unusual Christian character."
"He had the bearing and mind of a college or university-trained man," wrote the secretary of the faculty. "He was well balanced and energetic, possessing good judgment and considerable initiative. In his Practical Christian Work he proved to be a good speaker and an exceptionally good group-leader. . . . One official included in his estimate of John, 'he will undoubtedly be heard from'; another stated, 'expect to see this young man make good in a large way.'"

Unconscious of the opinions that were being formed of him, John found his studies the least taxing part of the new life. Many meetings for prayer were carried on among the students, both publicly and privately, amounting, indeed, to hundreds every month, but to guard his own quiet time of waiting upon God every morning he found to be a difficulty. Yet his spiritual life flagged and everything became mechanical if he missed that soul-renewing hour alone with God. To secure it, he had to rise at five, or soon after, and that he did with great steadfastness. Those around him felt the uplift of his reality in spiritual things. "John was one of the few among the student body whose life in a public way inspired my own growth in grace," writes one. But to the brother who was his chief correspondent, John confided, "My only trouble is myself."

The subject of the victorious life occupied his thoughts a good deal at this time. A talk in the Missionary Union one night greatly impressed him, and he sent the following notes to his brother:

> There is a platform known as Exposure to Temptation, and all men stand there. From it, each one goes either up or down.

SEVEN AWFUL STEPS DOWNWARD

1. Trifling with sin.

23

2. Yielding to sin.
3. Habitual yielding to sin.
4. Abandonment to sin: Ephesians 4:19.
5. Abandonment of God to sin: Romans 1:28.
6. Entering into alliance with the Devil to tempt others to sin.
7. Hell: and you do not have to die in order to get there. Hell is character as well as location. The man who hates everything that God loves is in Hell now, and Hell is in him.

SEVEN GLORIOUS STEPS UPWARD

1. Resistance as an attitude: determining that sin shall not have dominion over you.
2. Overcoming sin, by faith in Christ.
3. Habitual victory over sin. The strength that comes from one victory helps in overcoming the next temptation.
4. Learning the secret of a victorious life, a life "hid with Christ in God."
5. Taken up by God into deeper fellowship. You trusted God, and now God trusts you. "O Daniel, greatly beloved," yet he was only a man!
6. Made a succorer of others: like "the shadow of a great rock in a weary land."
7. Heaven: and you do not have to die in order to get there. Heaven is character as well as location. The man who devotedly loves everything that God loves is in Heaven now, and Heaven is in him.

I think, sometimes, we excuse ourselves when we fail, because we realize that the flesh is weak, If we could really see sin as God sees it, what a fight would be put up!

But it is a fight of *faith*. John knew his only source of strength. "Reckon, reckon, reckon rather than feel," he quotes from another teacher. "You take care of the reckoning, and God will make it real."

His prayer life was deepening, but not without cost.

For trials were permitted in the matter of financial supplies, greater even than he had anticipated. It was with this in mind that he wrote to his missionary brother in the Belgian Congo:

> The Lord has wonderfully taken care of me all through my stay here at Moody's. I count it a great privilege to be here, if only for the lessons I have learned of Him and of His dealings with men. . . . The classroom work is blessed, but I think I have learned even more outside of classes than in them.

He learned, for one thing, that the Lord has unexpected ways of caring for His children, and that the poor may be used as well as the rich in meeting needs known only to Him. He wrote from China later on:

> Is Mrs. C. still living? I'll never forget the two dollars that faithful woman sent me while I was at Moody's—and that, out of her own small earnings, peddling things from door to door. Truly, "of such is the kingdom of heaven."

It was not easy for John to accept gifts of this sort. He was independent and eager to work his way as far as possible. He served tables three times a day, when eight or nine hundred students took their meals together, and with so much success that, later on, he was made superintendent of the dining hall and even of the kitchen! But that work, though strenuous, brought small financial returns. And time was so occupied with assignments and study that he could not take a more remunerative position, though occasional chances came his way for office work. So he had the very thing he desired in going to Chicago, opportunity to prove for himself the reality of prayer and the dependability of the promises of God.

Very fresh in his mind was one experience, when he

wrote from China of his first Christmas at the Bible Institute. A fellow student from Paterson who was driving home for the holidays had offered him a seat in his car, but the journey would be cold and John's finances were low.

I had told Tom I was going with him, but I didn't have any money, and couldn't even buy a warm pair of socks for the trip home in the car. Then, one night, I pulled on one of the four shirts I had been planning to take home with me, and it ripped. I did not want to take home a mended shirt, for Mother would guess that finances were low, and I did want to see the Lord's provision, as a test of what His care would be in times to come.

I went out by the lake, feeling a bit blue and downcast, and found myself thinking:

"Well, it's all right to trust the Lord, but I wouldn't mind having a few dollars in my pocket."

Like a flash, I could have kicked myself! To think that I was valuing a few dollars in my pocket above the Lord's ability to provide a million if I needed it.

A few minutes later, just as I was crossing Michigan Boulevard—and jay-walking, too, which one is not supposed to do—I picked up a five-dollar bill from the street. Oh, what a rebuke it was from the Lord! Just one of those gentle rebukes the Lord can so wonderfully give us. The five dollars was beautifully acceptable, even though it was wet. I dried it out, and next day visited Montgomery Ward's bargain counter, and bought a couple of shirts and a good warm pair of socks, just the thing for the trip.

I am wearing those same socks still, and every time I pull them on, these cold nights, they preach a sermon on the Lord's wonderful power to provide, whatever my future needs may be.

At another time John's heart was touched by a very small happening, bringing a vivid sense of the nearness and care of God. He had to make an important telephone call, and took with him the five-cent piece that seems to have been about the last cash he had at the time. But the conversation resulted in his having to make a second call, and he had not the money. Distressed, he did not know what to do. But just then his eye fell upon an extra nickel in the telephone slot, just waiting to be used.

Trivial, surely! Only a five-cent piece that somebody had forgotten. But it was there when I needed it badly. And God, who knows each sparrow's hopping, knows our little needs too.

Those and other such experiences were so precious that he could not help sharing them with fellow students, not a few of whom were helped in their own difficulties by his attitude of joyous confidence and praise. It comes out, too, in some of his letters. To one about whose spiritual condition he was much concerned, John wrote:

Oh, I know you used to laugh at me! And you did scare me a bit the first time you called me into the office and gave me that lecture on what you thought of Christianity. But it did one thing for me. I went right down to Liggett's Drug Store, picked up a copy of Tom Paine's *Age of Reason*, got books on the alleged errors and contradictions of Holy Scripture, etc., and came away from the study more than ever convinced that the Bible is the Word of God.

Since then, I have been able to test the Bible in a practical way. I have seen its promises vindicated when God has heard and answered my prayers dozens of times, when no one could have known my situation, and when the supply tallied so wonderfully with the need that it was manifestly the hand of God.

Then, too, I have seen Him work in the lives of men. It's great to see men turn from their sins to seek the true

27

and living God, and to find in Him forgiveness and power to live a new life. Believe me, I would sooner be the most humble Christian, than have all a man could want of earthly things and yet be without Christ. I well remember how you used to say that all you wanted was money; you could purchase happiness with that. Perhaps you have found out your mistake already. If not, you surely will. . . . If you come to Christ for forgiveness and cleansing, He will give deliverance from the craving for sinful things, and will give you real peace and happiness in life. Oh, He is a wonderful Saviour and Lord, and a wonderful Master to work for!

Along another line also John's faith was being tested and he was becoming more and more sure of God. As often happens in the experience of young Christians, he was faced with perplexities in the matter of guidance. His outlook upon life was broadening. Many missionary speakers came to Moody, and he was studying missionary letters with increasing interest and making use of them in the meetings for which he was responsible. All that meant a fresh and strong appeal to give his own life to what we call "the foreign field." But his family did not seem to encourage such a course. His father had spared him to go to the Bible Institute in the definite hope that he would return to take up the work of the Star of Hope in Paterson. The time was coming when the mission would need a younger leader, and John was manifestly suited to such a post. Although holding all his children at God's disposal, and rejoicing that one son was at work in Equatorial Africa, Mr. Stam was deeply impressed with the conviction that "every man's life is a plan of God," and that young people should not overlook the need at home, or be swayed by merely human influences or personal desires in their choice of a lifework. John's love and respect for his father were so real that he could not but be troubled by that attitude of discouragement, felt rather than expressed. He wrote to his brother Jacob:

> The Lord knows where He wants me, whether in Holland, in Paterson or some other place in the States, in China, or in India. However, it does look frightfully disproportionate to see so many here in comparison with the few over yonder. We know that the Lord's work is not overstaffed here, but, as someone has said, "There are those who simply cannot go and those who are free to go. Why should both stay at home for the same work?"

The only thing he could do about it was pray. And as he prayed, he found that God was working. There was a gradual change of tone in his father's letters. At first he had written of his fear that sometimes "speakers and missionary societies try to persuade young people, through emotions, to choose the foreign work."

Then it was: "Why think of China or India, when there are other countries more open? Would it not seem more in keeping with the Lord's will to go where work can be unhindered, rather than where life is always in danger and there is so much opposition?"

And finally, nine months later: "May the Lord richly bless you and guide you by His Holy Spirit to do His will. We must pray that more men may go to China."

Conditions in China were undoubtedly serious at that time —June 1930. Communist armies were in possession of the larger part of Kiangsi and were making that beautiful and populous province run with blood. Three associate members of the China Inland Mission (now Overseas Missionary Fellowship) had suffered death at their hands, and two others were still held in captivity.

> It is an amazing thing that the provinces in China which are having most trouble are the very provinces in

which the China Inland Mission has, after prayerful consideration, decided to press forward evangelistic efforts. Two of their most valued workers, Mr. and Mrs. R. W. Porteous, are still in the hands of bandits, but reports have come through that they are teaching and preaching daily among their captors. It is said that the Communist soldiers like them so well that they declare that "these old people are too good to kill." They wish they would become Communists! With all its internal troubles, there seem to be unparalleled opportunities in China.

The very day after John wrote those words, Mr. and Mrs. Porteous were wonderfully liberated, brought back from the dead, it seemed, after a hundred days of suffering and peril.

3

A Home in China

FAR AWAY FROM CHICAGO was another home, very different
in its surroundings from the one to which John
owed so much. It was the rich background of another
young life —the life destined to complete his own. How
little either of them thought of this when they first met
at the Moody Bible Institute!

Elisabeth Alden Scott, born in the United States, had
been brought up in China, her parents being devoted
missionaries under the Presbyterian Board, USA. Directly descended from John and Priscilla Alden of the
Mayflower, she was of staunch New England ancestry.
Her father, Dr. Charles Ernest Scott, after a distin-
guished university career, had turned away from open-
ings in church and college to accept, with his young
wife, the hardships of home missionary work in the
woods of Michigan. They ministered also in the town
of Albion, where Betty was born, before sailing for
China, under appointment to evangelistic work and
Bible teaching. How strenuous and rewarding have
been their labors in the northern province of Shantung
is well known through Dr. Scott's writings and missionary addresses. Their influence as parents, though

not so widely known, enters vitally into this record, for all their children, by the blessing of God, have devoted their lives to His service and to China.[1]

In early years Elisabeth, the eldest, was characterized by simple winsomeness and warmth of love. When her father was at home, for example, she would slip quietly to his study door.

"What do you want, Betty?" he might question, recognizing the gentle little knock.

"I just want to tell you that I love you, Daddy!"

Then, made happy by a kiss, she would run off to play.

Betty's sister described their home.

Those were extraordinarily happy years for all of us—five little children in the beautiful city of Tsingtao, fairly living on the seashore. Betty and I got a great deal of pleasure out of trying to ride an antiquated bicycle of our father's. We were out of doors almost constantly, exploring and making our own the beautiful wooded country around us. We were all taught in an open-air sort of study, by a cousin who came to live with us for that purpose, until Betty went away to boarding school near Peking. Shortly after this we moved to Tsinan.

I think that our father and mother must have taken their career as parents more seriously than most people; for as we look back upon it all—the careful training, the many activities they shared with us, and the mental attitudes they so carefully instilled—we marvel at the work they must have put into it.

Our family motto was, "Do it together." At eleven o'clock every morning, no matter how busy Father might be—and he *was* busy—we all ran out and played hard at running games in the open air until our midday dinner, even Mother often sharing with us. After breakfast we had family prayers, each child choosing in turn the songs we sang and taking turns also in praying.

Father believed firmly in the value of athletics, and for a long time we used to do exercises together as soon as we were up in the morning, my brother blowing a trumpet to wake us. After early supper we had a reading hour, when Father or Mother read to us from beautifully illustrated children's books. Everyone was required to lie down after dinner, even when we were well grown. So all day long we were doing things together, and as there were scarcely any children of our own age within three miles of us, a strong family spirit developed.

One by one the children followed Betty to the coeducational school at Tungchow, where their studies were pursued for some years.

As I remember Betty then she was a gay, laughing, clever girl, with several boy admirers and many good friends among the girls. To me, the little sister, she was tender and thoughtful, and I recall many Sunday afternoons when we wandered round the campus with arms about each other, talking of home and school interests. We went home at Christmas and also every summer, when the family migrated to our cottage at Peitaiho, another seashore resort. There we spent most of the time swimming, playing tennis, reading, and acting as secretaries to Daddy, who was always loaded with work.

Sundays were strict but happy days. In earlier years they had neither church nor Sunday school to go to, save the long Chinese services which they did not usually attend. But their spiritual life was fed and inspired by the teaching and example of their parents at home. How deeply they had entered into Betty's life may be seen from lines she wrote long after, far from the sheltering care of those dear parents:

33

To Father and Mother

My words, dear Father, precious Mother,
　　May God select from His rich store.
I am, because you loved each other —
　　Oh, may my love unite you more!

When I was born, brimmed the bright water,
　　For pain and joy, in eyes gray-blue.
(A tiny bud of you, a daughter;
　　And yet, distinct, a person too!)

In pain and joy and love up-welling,
　　You treasured me against your heart;
And I, bewildered beyond telling,
　　Grew calm and slept, with tears astart.

As life grew bigger, I stood firmer,
　　With legs apart, eyes round and wide.
You told me all I asked, a learner
　　Who was not ever satisfied!

Throughout my childhood flitted fairies
　　Of sunshine and the open air,
Came chubby sisters, cheeked with cherries,
　　And baby boys with kewpie-hair.

We grew like colts and April saplings —
　　Seeking rebelliously for Truth.
You loved and learned and stood beside us,
　　And understood the shocks of youth.

As life grew mystical and magic
　　And I walked dreamily on earth,
Ere I should wake to see the tragic,
　　You planted, deep, ideals of worth.

You fed my mind, a flamelet tiny,
　　Yet keen and hungry, in a wood;

It seized and glowed and spread and crackled,
  And all the fuel in reach was good.

Somewhere beneath the loam of senses,
  A seed of Art you hoped was there,
Received the sun and rain and blossomed,
  All through your stimulating care.

But not content with mental culture,
  Seeing my spirit mourn in night,
You taught the Word and Way for sinners,
  Until Christ's Spirit brought me light.

Your loving courage never faltered,
  Your plans were gently laid aside,
(That time my whole life-pattern altered)
  Obedient to our Lord and Guide.

Your life for others, in each other,
  Shines through the world, pain-tarnished here;
As faithful stewards, Father, Mother,
  Your crown shall be unstained by tear.

Imagine, in God's certain Heaven,
  Your children made forever glad,
Praising the Lord for having given
  The dearest parents ever had.

Hard partings came when family life had to be broken up and the children sent to America to continue their education. Betty was almost ready for college when she was seventeen, and happily Dr. Scott's furlough was due, and they were able to go home all together. That journey had been long planned — six glorious months of study and travel, visiting Egypt, the Holy Land, Greece, Italy, Switzerland, France, and England.

35

It was a wonderful experience and we have hardly stopped talking about it since. All of us kept voluminous diaries and were thrilled to the core by every fresh experience. Of course the Holy Land was the most moving, seeing the Garden Tomb and the hill of Calvary. Other things one specially remembers are eating chocolate as we tramped and sang over mountain roads in Switzerland; walking on glaciers; climbing the Jungfrau; seeing Vesuvius; galloping on donkeys across the plains of Egypt, to visit the Tombs of the Kings; seeing an ancient pageant in Venice in honor of Mussolini; exploring cathedrals and picture galleries; visiting St. Peter's while the Pope was canonizing a new saint; almost losing our little brother, in hair-breadth escapes, and literally scores of other things.

One of the deepest impressions that came to Betty on this journey was made by a young Irishman who joined our party for several weeks and became like a big brother. We all adored him! But on Betty he made a special impression, as she did on him. He was leaving a worldly family to go as a missionary to Africa, and his consecration to Christ as well as his overflowing life and good spirits greatly attracted her. They corresponded a little after we separated, but in time lost touch with each other.

All five of us children expected at that time to return to China as missionaries. Our parents never urged it, but it seemed the natural and right thing to do. Our relations with the Chinese had been restricted but very friendly. Our Chinese servants were devoted Christian people and we loved them. We used to sneak out to their rooms, sometimes, to get the Chinese food which Mother thought not very good for us! The old *amah* who took care of us, and bossed us too, was specially dear. At school we had little contact with anyone outside the campus, but Betty and I both studied Chinese characters for two years, writing as well as reading, expecting to need it later on.

So all the family came home in 1923. For Betty, it was the joyous ending of childhood's years. And the way looked bright before her. The eager delight she took in life at this time may be gathered from her "Traveller's Song":

I sought for beauty on the earth,
    And found it everywhere I turned;
        A precious stone from Singapore
        That sapphire shone and sapphire burned —
A Rajah's ransom it was worth.

Eternal grandeur brooded deep
    In Egypt's pyramids of stone,
        And still I smell the orange bloom;
    I see the frosty stars that shone
And cooled the tranquil Nile to sleep.

I loved the skies of Italy,
    The swarthy, singing boatmen there,
        The Virgins of the Renaissance,
    With grave, sweet eyes and golden hair —
The land of Art and Melody.

Lingers long into the night
    On snowy peaks the Alpine glow,
        And every lake is loveliest,
    And there, amid the endless snow,
I picked the edelweiss so white.

Before a Chinese city gate,
    The entrance to an ancient town,
        I saw the men fly dragon-kites;
    While, by the willows weeping down,
Their wives beat clothes, from dawn till late.

Then home I came, as though on wings,
    The joy of life in heart and eyes;

For, everything was glorified —
The earth, the ocean, and the skies,
And even all the common things!

¹"Elisabeth and Beatrice have already gone to China," wrote Dr. Courtenay
H. Fenn of the Presbyterian Board, "Elisabeth to lay down her life heroically
with her husband; Beatrice as the wife of Dr. Theodore Stevenson in our
South China Mission. Helen with her husband, the Rev. George Gordon
Mahy, Jr., after several years of service in Witherspoon College, Kentucky.
Francis, now a student in Princeton Seminary, and his younger brother
Kenneth, in Davidson College, are also planning for the mission field. Hav-
ing seen considerable of their home life in China, I gladly bear testimony to
the beauty of the family relations and the fine training received by the
children."

4

College and Deeper Things

ALMOST A YEAR LATER Betty entered Wilson College, Chambersburg, Pennsylvania, with a large freshman class, but it was a very different Betty from the one who had climbed the Alps and soared on wings of expectation. For while at high school for a few months, she had been struck down with sudden and serious illness. Inflammatory rheumatism had run its painful course, leaving her with a heart so weakened that she had to lie flat on her back for months, even after the worst was over. Happily her parents had not yet returned to China. Happily also, her faith was rooted in the love of God. But they had been long, hard months, brightened chiefly by the gifts that came to her. For it was at that time she discovered that she could write poetry. It was then also that spiritual things became real in a new way.

So it was natural that the point of view Betty brought to college life should be different from that of other girls of her age. Though only eighteen, she had seen much of the world and had had unusual experiences. Her outlook was wide, and her feelings ran deep. Above all, divine realities had come to mean much to her.

Smoking, dancing, and other frivolities had no appeal to such a life, and Betty was set down by many as "one of those religious people" of whom they were inclined to fight shy. But a couple of years later, when Helen joined her, those first difficulties had been overcome.

By that time Betty had carved out real respect for herself on two scores—her literary gifts, which were admitted to be more than ordinary, and the depth and sincerity of her religious life. She was president of her literary society, and editor (associate) of the literary publication, interested also in dramatics, and an active Student Volunteer. She was acknowledged to be one of the finest students in her class, graduating with a *Magna Cum Laude*.

We were very close together at this time. Betty was interested in everything I went in for, especially athletics, which her heart condition would not let her take up, and she rejoiced in my little victories even more than I did.

Some of Betty's contributions to the college magazine give glimpses of the soul of an artist as well as poet. Her love of the beautiful comes out in her lines entitled "Color," every one of which is a picture. Part only can be quoted:

"Color? What's color?" "Friend, now listen well,
While I some bits of color bring for you."
"Color is meaningless: I pray thee, tell
The use of yellow, red and blue."
"Friend, you have eyes, but you are blind:
Color is sight and feeling, heart, and mind.

"The blue Swiss lakes, with lighter skies above;
A dewy, crimson rosebud, sign of love;
An Irish child with red-gold tangled curls;
A jet-haired prima donna, decked with pearls;
Deep fields of goldenrod in early fall;

And purple asters by an old stone wall;
An Indian blanket, black and red and green;
A 'nut-brown maiden' in peach gingham seen.

"Wistaria in a rain-fresh, drooping mass;
A cardinal, flashing blithely o'er the grass;
An ancient Bible, purple vellum bound,
With silver letters and designs around;
A campfire, ruddy, golden, blue-tipped, bright,
Touching the vague woods round with flickering light;
The joyous forms of angels, long ago
Wrought piously by Fra Angelico.

"An apple tree, just bursting into bloom;
A rug of Chinese blue from Orient loom;
The rainbow spray that gleams o'er Giesbach Falls;
Venetian moonlight on old palace walls;
A sunset in the tropics, salmon pink,
With silhouetted palms, as black as ink;
The scarlet poppies, gay in the mountain breeze,
'Neath ancient, twisted, gray-green olive trees.

"A field of waving daffodils, the poet's joy;
A jaunty U.S. Navy sailor boy;
An ancient Chinese green-bronze temple bell;
The pearly pinkish lining of a shell;
A sweet Madonna robed in blue and red;
The golden curls upon Apollo's head;
The high priest's breastplate, with its wondrous gems;
The lights of London rippling in the Thames.

"The mummy gods; Osiris, bluish green,
The judge of spirits, on tomb-walls oft seen;
The cloak that Raleigh threw for good Queen Bess,
Red velvet, broidered thick with pearls, I guess;
A little black-haired flapper, just nineteen,
In taf'ta dancing frock of apple green,
Trimmed with French flowers, silver, rose and cream."

"Enough! I have been blind, but now I see.
Henceforth the world holds richer stores for me."

There are poems also that betray the happy, fun-loving side of Betty's nature. What a bubbling over of life we find, for instance, in "A Jingle of Words"!

Don't you love the common words
    In usage all the time;
Words that paint a masterpiece,
    Words that beat a rhyme,
Words that sing a melody,
    Words that leap and run,
Words that sway a multitude,
    Or stir the heart of one?

Don't you love the lively words —
    Flicker, leap and flash,
Tumble, stumble, pitch and toss,
    Dive, and dart and dash,
Scramble, pirouette and prance,
    Hurtle, hurdle, fling,
Waddle, toddle, trot and dance,
    Soar and snatch and swing?

Don't you love the lengthy words —
    Subterranean,
Artificial, propagate,
    Neapolitan,
Revelation, elevate,
    Ambidextrous
Undenominational,
    Simultaneous?

Don't you love the noisy words —
    Clatter, pop and bang,
Scrape and creak and snarl and snort,
    Crash and clash and clang,
Crackle, cackle, yowl and yap,

Snicker, snare and sneeze,
Screech and bellow, slash and howl,
Whistle, whine and wheeze?

Don't you love the colorful —
Amber, rose and gold,
Orchid, orange and cerise,
Crimson, emerald,
Purple, plum and lavender,
Peach and Prussian blue,
Turquoise matrix, jade and jet,
Hazel, honeydew?

Yes, with just the common words
In usage everywhere,
You can capture incidents
Beautiful and rare.
In words you have a weapon
More mighty than a gun;
You can sway the multitude
Or stir the heart of one.

But it was in higher things that Betty's influence was
most felt. Dr. Nevius of the faculty at Wilson wrote:

It seems only yesterday that Betty herself was here, in
the classroom, as a Student Volunteer, at her post in the
Cabinet, and in her literary society; with her gentle,
gracious presence, exerting that quiet and pervasive influence for which she will always be remembered by
those who knew her. . . .

To recall her to those who shared with her any one of
the four happy years of college life, is to recall a presence so radiant of sincerity and inward beauty that its
memory can never be effaced. Perhaps what most
alumnae will remember, aside from the gentleness of
her demeanor, the fragrance of her loving spirit and the
grace of her literary expression, will be the serenity and
faith with which she lived among us; a serenity born of

the deep peace of her own soul, and a faith that was founded upon a Rock. Values like this cannot perish.

It was before her second year at college that Betty came to know the exchanged life, the life that is "not I but Christ," in a new and fuller way. After attending a summer conference at Keswick, New Jersey, she wrote to her parents from an overflowing heart:

"Keswick" is over, but I trust never the message! Thank the Lord! I have now surrendered myself to the Lord more than I have ever realized was possible. Already He has wonderfully answered my prayers, in little things and in big ones. Nearly all the most unlikely boys and girls were won to consecrate their lives to Him. The "Say-So Meeting" yesterday was simply triumphant. I have never realized that such victory was possible. The Way is just Christ—and complete consecration to His will in our lives. Among other things, I have dedicated to Him whatever I have of poetic or literary gift. Maybe He can use me along that line. Wouldn't it be wonderful! I have been greatly impressed by the way in which Mr. Harkness had dedicated his musical talents to the Lord.

Giving my life to Jesus makes me see what I ought to have done long ago, and I wonder how I can have been so dumb before. Now that sounds as though I were a perfect little angel, flapping my wings 'round! But, of course, I'm awfully imperfect still, or as one might put it, future-perfect—which means that there is promise for the future. Even now, when I put first the pleasure, interests and point of view of others, everything goes along most gaily. "Keswick" has been a wonderful revelation to me of how victorious the victorious life really is. Since being there I have had my prayers answered in most definite ways. Now the Lord is showing me how necessary it is to rise early in the morning to read His Word, and He is helping me to wake and get up in time to do so.

I don't know what God has in store for me. I really am willing to be an old-maid missionary, or an old-maid anything else, all my life, if God wants me to. It's as clear as daylight to me that the only worth-while life is one of unconditional surrender to God's will, and of living in His way, trusting His love and guidance.

A year later, still facing the tests of college life, she was able to add on this vital subject:

There is nothing unpractical or disappointing about seeking to live victoriously and happily in Christ, provided you don't try so hard, but just trustfully let Him live. I was much impressed yesterday in reading that when God consecrated Aaron and his sons for the priesthood He literally "filled their hands" for a whole week (Leviticus 8:33).[1] When we consecrate ourselves to God, we think we are making a great sacrifice, and doing lots for Him, when really we are only letting go some little, bitsie trinkets we have been grabbing, and when our hands are empty, He fills them full of His treasures.

It was at this "Keswick" that Betty took as her life motto the glorious assurance: "To me to live is Christ, and to die is gain." It was at this "Keswick" also that she began to pray that, if it were God's will, nothing might prevent her from returning to China as a missionary.

With this hope in view, Betty decided, upon leaving college, to go to Chicago for practical training at the Moody Bible Institute. Her sister tells us,

She chose Moody's because she wanted to learn how to win souls to Christ, instead of just talking about it theoretically, or discussing the Bible in an abstract way. The course at Moody's gave her great spiritual poise, and the prison and street meetings, which her sensitive spirit had dreaded, turned out to be a help and brought her no little joy.

Plunged into the life of a great institution and the pressure of a crowded schedule, Betty found new meaning in her recent act of faith. In the rush of things in Chicago, could it be practically true, "to me to live is Christ"? The instinctive turning of her heart to God finds expression in lines written soon after she entered the Bible school.

O Jesus Christ, Thou Son of God and Son of man,
Thy love no angel understands, nor mortal can!

Thy strength of soul, Thy radiant purity,
Thine understanding heart of sympathy,
The vigor of Thy mind, Thy poetry,
Thy heavenly wisdom, Thy simplicity,
Such sweetness and such power in harmony!

Thy perfect oneness with Thy God above;
The agony endured to show Thy love!
Thou who didst rise triumphantly to prove
Thou art the Living God, before whom death
And Hell itself must shake and move!

Thou Son of God —
Grant me Thy face to see,
Thy voice to hear, Thy glory share;
Never apart from Thee,
Ever Thine own to be,
Throughout eternity.

With such an inward life, it is interesting to see how this girl impressed others among the hundreds of her fellow students. Of those, her chief friends went to China, too far away to be available for this record, but those who knew her less intimately write:

Betty was quiet, never profuse, gently direct, and above the average in intelligence and culture. She was never hurried or ruffled. Her dress, while suited to the occasion, was never the least bit showy. For classes, she usually wore low Oxfords, a dark blue sport skirt, and a sweater of plain style and the darker hues. She did not wear jewelry or frills and flowers. Her dark, straight hair, parted on one side, was worn in a knot at the back of the neck. I thought this very becoming to her, with her lovely, rather rounded face. Her voice and expression were soft, pleasing and gentle. She was well built and well poised. Her choice was evidently the simple life, with high ideals and a definite goal.

Betty was one of the outstanding young women at Moody's.
I admired the zeal and sweetness of her life. . . . Betty had that unmistakable confidence in the Lord and Christlike spirit which never failed to help those who came to know her. It was clear that her opinions were formed only after serious thought and definite prayer.

Nothing was more characteristic of Betty Scott, as time went on, than the depth and sincerity of her prayer life, especially in relation to others. She was learning that it is better to pray than to criticize, to "supply"[2] than to dwell upon deficiencies. And what a test of growth in spiritual things that is! Her "Sonnet on Prayer" shows something of this development. It is based on Jeremiah 31:12, "Their soul shall be as a watered garden."

I passed a thorny desert soul one day,
A soul as fruitless as a painted mast —
So harsh and hard and dry I stood aghast,
And would have helped, but had no time to stay,
Yet, half in doubtfulness, began to pray
To Him the Source of living streams. At last,

47

Returning, I beheld a velvet-grassed,
Abundant garden; saw the rainbow spray
Of fountains, shimm'ring high against the trees;
Saw old-time flowers, pansies and sweet peas,
Pink-hearted phloxes, heliotrope, heartsease.
Clustering roses hung from arches there;
The scent of hidden orchards filled the air,
And there were children's voices everywhere.

Few, even among Betty's friends realized how searching were some of the experiences that came to her during these years in Chicago. Her outward calm gave little
indication of the deepening work of God within. "It
almost seemed," her father wrote, "as though, out of
her peaceful, sheltered life, she had prescience of terrible things she would some day encounter for the Lord,
and be called upon to suffer for His dear sake. Meanwhile, her leal heart was in training for the tragic test."
Part of her exercise of mind was due to uncertainty as
to her future field of service. Her heart called her to
China, but she feared that it was partly love of parents
and home that influenced her. Africa came before her at
that time, and especially the need of its suffering lep-
ers, for whom there seemed so few to care. Could she be
willing to give up all that China meant, and consecrate
her life to so Christlike yet painful a task? With Betty's
direct nature, the question had to be answered. She
faced it fully, and though it meant death to her loving,
aesthetic nature, she was enabled to offer herself even
for that, if it were the will of God. "My Testimony" is
the title she gives to some revealing lines:

And shall I fear
That there is anything that men hold dear
Thou would'st deprive me of,
And nothing give in place?

That is not so —

48

For I can see Thy face
And hear Thee now:

"My child, I died for thee.
And if the gift of love and life
You took from Me,
Shall I one precious thing withhold—
One beautiful and bright
One pure and precious thing withhold?
My child, it cannot be."

Yet the testings had to go deeper, before that true and
eager soul was satisfied in its following hard after God.
Consecration meant much more to her now than it had
even at Keswick, five years previously. To her father the
following verses were sent in her second year at
Moody:

"This poem," she wrote, "expresses the distress of
soul and fear of mind that were mine before I surrendered my all—even inmost motives, so far as I know—
to God's control. The fourth stanza is His gracious acceptance of my unworthy self; the last tells of the joy,
satisfaction, and peace of assured guidance that Christ
my Saviour gives me, now that He is Lord of my life."

STAND STILL AND SEE

I'm standing, Lord:
There is a mist that blinds my sight.
Steep, jagged rocks, front, left and right,
Lower, dim, gigantic, in the night.
    Where is the way?

I'm standing, Lord:
The black rock hems me in behind,
Above my head a moaning wind
Chills and oppresses heart and mind.
    I am afraid!

49

I'm standing, Lord:
The rock is hard beneath my feet;
I nearly slipped, Lord, on the sleet.
So weary, Lord! and where a seat?
    Still must I stand?

He answered me, and on His face
A look ineffable of grace,
Of perfect, understanding love,
Which all my murmuring did remove.

    I'm standing, Lord:
Since Thou hast spoken, Lord, I see
Thou hast beset — these rocks are Thee!
And since Thy love encloses me,
    I stand and sing.

Was this experience permitted in order that its sur-
passing consolation might come back to her on another
night, some shadow of which seems already to have
fallen across her pathway?

---

¹Revised Version, margin.
²Ephesians 4:15-16: "That which every joint supplieth."

5

A Discovery

B ETTY HAD ALREADY BEEN a year at Moody Bible Institute
when John appeared among the students. His tall
figure could not but attract attention. Betty noticed
him; and about her, quiet and retiring as she was, he
soon discovered something he had never found before,
something that strangely attracted him. How do we dis-
cover violets hidden in the woods in spring?

The weekly prayer meeting of the China Inland Mission was partly responsible for the deepening of this
friendship. It was held on Monday evenings in the
home of Mr. and Mrs. Isaac Page, representatives of the
mission in the Midwest. Themselves devoted and en-
thusiastic missionaries, Mr. and Mrs. Page had much to
give to students and others interested in China. Betty
was one of the regular attendants—for by that time her
call to China was unmistakable—and John was soon
found among their number. Sometimes after the meetings there would be a social hour, when refreshments
were served and Mr. Page might introduce one or
another of his favorite books. He loved to read from
Samuel Rutherford's Letters, already precious to John,
and "never shall I forget," he recalls, "the look in Betty

51

Scott's eyes as I repeated those wonderful verses on Immanuel's Land."

In the busy life of the Institute, the young people only met as fellow students, and so natural was their behavior that no one guessed that they had any special interest in each other. John's time was much taken up with practical work in addition to his studies, especially after he assumed the care of a church in a rural district which was without a minister. Two hundred miles from Chicago, it seemed a long way to go once or twice a month, to care for that little group of hungry-hearted people. But how worthwhile it was may be judged from their own loving testimony:

> We shall always remember his first appearance in our pulpit, and how pleased we were with his earnest message. His kind, courteous manner, his zeal and fresh enthusiasm and his helpful sermons won us completely. To reach our little town of Elida, Ohio, he had to travel some two hundred miles. His remuneration was very little, yet his interest in and affection for us were greater than the difficulties, and he remained our faithful pastor until he was graduated from the Bible Institute.

The church was a small building out in the country, surrounded by a farming population. John was entertained over the weekends with all the hospitality the members could afford. It was a refreshment to leave the city, even in winter, and his Elida friends remember his delight in the sky and stars that the glare of Chicago painfully obscured. The work was not without its hardships and discouragements, but he took it as a test to see whether he "could ever do anything for the Lord in China." That he deeply felt his own insufficiency comes out in letters written at the time, as also his growing confidence in God:

Why should we not yield our fruit in season, and why should it not be with us as with the man in the first Psalm, "Whatsoever he doeth shall prosper"? Is it too much to expect our God to do exceeding abundantly above? Can we put a strain on Omnipotence, or can we exhaust infinite Love? Lord, increase our faith!

Did the members of the little church realize how much travail of soul lay behind his ministry among them? That he was appreciated, perhaps more than he knew, is evident from their recollections:

He preached for us for more than sixteen months. We were impressed by his great earnestness. He wasted no time. We were reminded of the saying of Jonathan Edwards, "I am resolved, while I live, to live with all my might."

Mr. Stam was always reverent in the pulpit. We were never disappointed in his preaching. Not once did he let down in his prayerful, painstaking preparation. His sermons were scriptural, inspiring and concise, never tedious. His rule was to "Go" to the people in the community who did not attend services. This often led to long walks, that he might minister to Christians, Catholics, or unbelievers.

John was one of the finest young men. He loved his Bible and loved to tell of Jesus. He loved to come to the country and see God's wonderful handiwork in nature. He loved children, and would teach them Bible stories and many choruses. He loved to sing God's praises.

That singing made a great impression in Elida, for John had a good tenor voice and sometimes brought other students with him for special services. Once or twice they formed a quartet, and Elida people called them "The Happy Four."

And indeed they were always happy and singing on

their way. Their wonderful singing and addresses told us so plainly that they knew the power of the Gospel of Christ.

John was more than our minister. He not only taught and preached, he was our close and intimate friend also. He visited most if not all of us in our homes. He was quick to see a joke, and could be jolly and enjoy himself wherever he happened to be, especially where there were young folks and children. And they loved him greatly. I can see him still, when he came up to see our little granddaughters, then only three months old. He stood for some time looking down into the baskets in which they lay.

"Such little tots!" he said. "And you never can tell what lies before them in life."

He had a tender, understanding heart.

Best of all, he made the Word of God live for us. Every Sunday before the sermon, we had fifteen minutes of repeating Scripture from memory. Among his special Bible verses were: "Thou wilt keep him in perfect peace whose mind is stayed on thee," and, "The Lord is my helper, I will not fear what man shall do unto me."

Faithfulness was a theme he loved to dwell upon: both faithfulness in the Christian life and God's own faithfulness to us. How he could sing, "Great is Thy faithfulness!" Just to know him, to hear him sing God's praises, to be near him was such a privilege. His life was full of the promises of God, and we were so proud to have him for our friend!

Another recollection of Elida people is the way John would come back again and again to the assurance: "My God shall supply all your need according to his riches in glory by Christ Jesus." That he was still proving that to be true in his own experience is evident from a letter written at that time. He was concerned to see, as he thought, just a shade of anxiety in his father's references to the financial condition of the Star of Hope Mission. Supported by voluntary contributions, for no collections were ever taken, the work was entirely dependent upon God, through His people. John's interest in home affairs was as keen as ever, and in the spring, after his first visit to Elida (January, 1931) he wrote to his father with a good deal of diffidence:

> I would not mention what I am going to tell you now, if the Mission were not in the position it is; but I do want to give praise to God for the way He has led me during the past year. About twelve months ago, when I began to come to an end of the money I had taken to the Institute, I told the Lord that if I were to go to China I must know Him as the answerer of prayer here in the homeland. And the Lord has wonderfully shown Himself to me as Jehovah-jireh, and that right here in Chicago. Sometime, perhaps just before I leave for China, I may tell you some of these experiences. If I did not know before that God works today, just as of old, I know it now. And may I mention some of the lessons I have had to learn?

> First, that it is all of grace. God does not reward us with what we need, because of our faithfulness. We are unprofitable servants at the very, very best.

> Second, that it is useless to get down and pray unless we have searched the Word and let it search us (Psalm 139:23-24), even our thoughts toward others, our motives and desires. Once I had to wait three days for urgently needed help, to learn this lesson.

> Third, that it is not our faith we must depend on, but

God's faithfulness —our faith being only the hand held out to receive of His faithfulness.

Fourth, that if the answer does not seem to come, there may be something in me that causes God to delay in *very faithfulness*. His faithfulness causes Him *not* to answer me, in such a case. He cannot encourage His servant in a wrong attitude by answering his prayers, can He?

Fifth, the faith must be intelligently based upon the revealed will of God. Not because I have a supreme conviction that I need something or other, but because I find it is His will, I can pray with confidence.

Sixth, that I am not to expect the Lord to answer in just the way I suggest, or think best. Means and manner and everything must be left to the will of God. We keep on looking to our usual or possible sources of supply, forgetting that our real source of supply is the Lord, and that He can use anyone, anywhere, with equal ease and freedom.

How I do thank Him for this past year! I would not have had it otherwise, for all the ease of a bank balance. How could I ever have learned to trust the Lord, even a little, if everything had gone smoothly? How could He have checked me up, had I not been entirely dependent upon Him? Of course He knows what we need! We can have blessed peace and rest without anything at all to depend on but His promises. . . . The Book has become a new Book to me, this last year.

Oh, how blessed I have found that promise: "Seek ye first the kingdom of God, and his righteousness; and all these things shall be added unto you" (Matthew 6:33)! That's a business contract with two parties, God and ourselves. How poor would be our stay, if it were only

56

the supplies in sight, or the people who usually sent the money! But, the living God —can He forget His own work? It is not our work; it is His. His interest in it exceeds ours a thousandfold. As long as we are in His will, He cannot forget us. Could Mother forget her boys? Try as either you or Mother might, you could not forget us. . . .

Dear Dad, what a blessed thing it is that God thinks it worth while to test us! Workmen only spend time and trouble on materials they can make something out of. God will perfect that which concerns us, Hallelujah!

To one of his brothers John had written a few days before:

Take away anything I have, but do not take away the sweetness of walking and talking with the King of glory! It is good to let our thoughts run away with us, sometimes, concerning the greatness of our God and His marvelous kindness toward us. Looking back, what encouragement we find for the future, what wonderful leadings and providences! Oh, bless the Lord, my soul!

But there are always new testings to be faced, new opportunities of proving God, and such a time had come to John Stam now. For one thing, the call to China was more and more urgent.

A million a month pass into Christless graves over there. God can use us if only we are empty, broken vessels in His hand. Oh, how much more do we need preparation of heart and spirit than of the mind! Pray that I may have that.

Another question also was exercising his mind. For a great love had come into his life. John had never, in the years at home, preferred one girl friend above another. He had kept entirely free in heart and outward relations. He expected not only to go to China unmarried but to remain so for at least five years, as his hope was to engage in pioneering evangelistic work. The forward movement of the China Inland Mission appealed to him, and he was ready to offer for the mountain tribes of the west or the Muslims of Sinkiang. But now he faced a new situation. What did that great love mean? Was it a crowning gift that God was bringing into his life?

And Betty with her pure, sweet nature, did not hide from him that his love might be returned. Years before, when only a girl of eighteen, she had written with such a possibility in view:

My Ideal

I'll recognize my true love
  When first his face I see;
For he will strong, and healthy,
  And broad of shoulder be:
His movements will be agile,
  Quick, and full of grace;
The eyes of Galahad will smile
  Out of his friendly face.

His features won't be Grecian,
  Nor yet will they be rough;
His fingers will be flexible,
  Long, and strong, and tough:
Oh, he'll be tall, and active
  As any Indian,
With rounded muscles rippling out
  Beneath his healthy tan.

. . . .

His interest is boundless
  In every fellow man;

He'll gladly be a champion
   As often as he can:
Oh, he'll be democratic,
   And maybe shock the prude;
He will not fawn before the great,
   Nor to the low be rude.

He'll be a splendid "mixer,"
   For he has sympathy;
Perhaps his most pronouncèd trait
   Is versatility;
If Providence should drop him
   In any foreign town,
He'd somehow speak the language
   And find his way around.

He'll have a sense of humor
   As kindly as it's keen;
He'll be a mighty tower
   On which the weak may lean.
His patience and unselfishness
   May readily be seen;
He's very fond of children,
   And children worship him.

He will not be a rich man,
   He has no earthly hoard;
His money, time, heart, mind and soul
   Are given to the Lord,
He'll be a modern Daniel,
   A Joshua, a Paul;
He will not hesitate to give
   To God his earthly all.

He'll be, he'll be, my hero —
   A strong-armed fighting man,
Defender of the Gospel,
   And Christian gentleman.

Oh, if he asks a Question,
  My answer "Yes" will be!
For I would trust and cherish
  Him to eternity.

Had her girlish dream come true? How strangely her
picture-poem seemed to fit John Stam! But she found
much more in him than she had dreamed of then. Her
own life had deepened. Her ideal now was spiritual
fellowship, oneness of heart in the things of God. And
that too was satisfied in this friendship.

But the way was not as clear as it might seem. Betty's
last term at the Bible Institute had come. She was leaving Chicago and had applied for membership in the
China Inland Mission. If accepted, she would go out in
a few months. John had another year at Moody. He was
not sure yet about China. He hoped to join the China
Inland Mission but would have to pass a medical test
and be accepted by the director and council. All that
left room for uncertainty. He could not ask Betty to
commit herself to an engagement, when his way might
not open to follow her to China. And more than that,
even if his going proved to be of the Lord, what about
the life of hardship as a pioneer evangelist? He might
be in work that would preclude his marrying for some
years. Would it be fair to Betty to ask her to wait indefi-
nitely?

Had he known the steadfastness of her heart and her
capacity for unchanging devotion, he might not have
hesitated on that score. The other consideration, however, did appeal to Betty as to him. Her path was plain.
God had called her to China and had opened the way.
John's future was still uncertain. If health or other circumstances kept him at home, she could not turn back
from her lifework. They had seen something of the sorrow and loss that had come to others through not seek-

ing first the kingdom of God, through letting down spiritual standards and losing the heavenly vision.

So Betty went forward with her preparations, quietly leaving it all in the hands of God. Accepted by the China Inland Mission, she was to sail that fall of 1931. It was a comfort to them both that in crossing the continent she could spend a day in Chicago with John. And it happened to be a Monday. So they attended the prayer meeting together once more in the home of Mr. and Mrs. Page.

It had been a wonderful day, down by the lake, in hours of talk and prayer. They were parting for a long, long time, perhaps years. They were not engaged, hard though it was to leave each other so. "God first" was the attitude of their hearts. Nothing must come before that loyalty. Mr. Page recalled,

> Just before leaving for China Betty attended the prayer meeting with John. When it was over they wanted to talk with me, and John, in a very delightful way, tried to tell what was in his heart regarding Betty. He thought we had not noticed anything! Then, speaking for both of them, he said that they were leaving the matter in the Lord's hands, but felt that He was bringing them together.

How safe it is to leave our dearest interests there in His hands! To his father John had written:

> Betty knows that, in all fairness and love to her, I cannot ask her to enter into an engagement with years to wait. But we can have a real understanding, keeping the interests of the Lord's work always first.

> The China Inland Mission has appealed for men, single men, to itinerate in sections where it would be almost impossible to take a woman, until more settled work has been commenced. . . . Some time ago I prom-

ised the Lord that, if fitted for this forward movement, I would gladly go into it, so now I cannot back down without sufficient reason, merely upon personal considerations. If, after we are out a year or two, we find that the Lord's work would be advanced by our marriage, we need not wait longer.

From the way I have written, you and Mother might think that I was talking about a cartload of lumber, instead of something that has dug down very deep into our hearts. Betty and I have prayed much about this, and I am sure that, if our sacrifice is unnecessary, the Lord will not let us miss out on any of His blessings. Our hearts are set to do His will. . . . But this is true, isn't it, our wishes must not come first? The progress of the Lord's work is the chief consideration. So there are times when we just have to stop and think hard.

The parting was very near when that letter reached Paterson, and with a keen sense of all it meant, Father Stam exclaimed, "Those children are going to have God's choicest blessing!"

"When God is second," he added, "you will get second best; but when God is really first, you have His best."

6

A Surprise of Joy

EIGHT MONTHS HAD PASSED since the time of Betty's sailing for China, and she was already in an inland city when John completed his studies in Chicago. They had been long months for both of them, for uncertainty is one of the hardest things to bear. John had made application to the China Inland Mission but still had to pass the medical exam and be accepted by the director and council. So his way was not yet plain.

Meanwhile, his heart and conscience were increasingly burdened with the need of the non-Christian world. Chosen by his fellow students to give the class address at their graduation exercises, he put much prayer and preparation into his discourse. The class motto was "Bearing Precious Seed," and that he connected with the Lord's own words: "The field is the world." Deep and lasting was the impression made by that address with its challenging appeal to faith.

In politics, today, men are thinking in terms of international affairs. In business, all the continents are being combed for markets; and even in daily life, every newspaper reader is becoming world-conscious. And yet, we, the people of God, have not fully realized that we are to be a testimony to the world. . . . Heathen populations are growing in numbers daily, but we are not reaching them, much less matching their increasing numbers with increased efforts to bring them the Gospel. Not only are heathen populations growing —with the frontiers of civilization moving ahead and education advancing —idolatry and superstition are breaking down. Now is the time to reach men whose minds are swept of old beliefs, before communistic atheism, coming in like a flood, raises other barriers far harder to overcome, and before this generation passes into Christless graves.

Our own civilization also challenges us as Christian workers. This country, once so strong in its Christian testimony, is becoming increasingly godless. Our educational systems are sweeping us away from faith. Old standards of morality are fast going, and those great and holy truths, once so sacred, are becoming the butt of jokes to furnish humor for our periodicals.

Searching words followed on the condition of the church and the lack of joy and power in Christian testimony. "We have been guilty of acting more like the beleagured garrison of a doomed fortress than like soldiers of our ever-conquering Christ." A sober review was given of present depressing financial conditions, that bear so heavily upon all forms of Christian activity. Then the searchlight of faith was turned upon the whole situation, at home as well as abroad:

Shall we beat a retreat, and turn back from our high calling in Christ Jesus; or dare we advance at God's command, in face of the impossible? . . . Let us remind ourselves that the Great Commission was never qualified by clauses calling for advance only if funds were plentiful and no hardship or self-denial involved. On the contrary, we are told to expect tribulation and even persecution, but with it victory in Christ.

64

It is good to remember that that was no veteran speaking, but a young man moved by the constraining love of Christ, and one ready to seal his testimony with his blood. How our hearts should be stirred by the appeal of the young leaders God is giving us, here and in other lands, the hope and glory of our fast-closing age!

Friends, the task with all its attendant difficulties is enough to fill our hearts with dismay, if we look only to ourselves and our weakness. But the authority in our Master's command to go forward should fill us with joy and the expectation of victory. He knows our weakness and our lack of supplies. He knows the roughness of the way. And His command carries with it the assurance of all we need. Of course we want to be assured of our support! Who cares to go forward in any enterprise, secular or religious, unless he can be reasonably sure that it will not be dropped for lack of funds? Incomes are falling, men are losing employment, and bank accounts are being wiped out. Do we, as Christian workers, want to be sure of support? Then let us not put our trust in men, or in any God-dishonoring methods of raising funds for the work. These are not certain enough. We have it on the highest authority that the promise is of *faith*, that it might be sure. The faithfulness of God is the only certain thing in the world today. We need not fear the result of trusting Him. . . .

Our way is plain. We must not retrench in any work which we are sure is in His will and for His glory. We dare not turn back because the way looks dark. . . . We must go forward in the face of the impossible, even if we only know the next step. . . . We may find ourselves at the place where we shall have to drink the bitter waters of Marah, but our Captain's presence can sweeten the most bitter waters. We may come to the very last of our supplies, but He is still able to give us each day our daily bread. And what if we should, like Allen Gardiner, be permitted even to die of starvation?

Like him, we shall find our moments of suffering aglow with the sunshine of Christ's presence, and shall have nothing but praise for the grace and mercy bestowed upon us.

This bewildered age needs to know that only "the foundation of God standeth sure." Many a man is being torn loose, these days, from the things to which his heart has clung. It is ours to show the incorruptible riches which bank failures and economic conditions cannot touch. It is ours to show, in the salvation of our Lord Jesus Christ, and in personal communion with Him, a joy unspeakable and full of glory that cannot be affected by outside circumstances. . . .

Does it not thrill our hearts to realize that we do not go forward in our own strength! Think of it, God Himself is with us for our Captain! The Lord of Hosts is present in Person on every field of conflict, to encourage us and fight with us. With such a Leader, who never lost a battle, or deserted a soldier in distress, or failed to get through the needed supplies, who would not accept the challenge to go forward, "bearing precious seed"?

The attitude of John's classmates, several of whom went to China about the same time, is sufficient comment upon his life and influence in the Bible Institute. One of his friends wrote,

He was a prince among men. How we all admired him! And I love him as I have loved few others.

He had a passion for souls. His personal work was exemplary, in that he was always at it. . . . John was not ascetic in any way. One could have plenty of fun on a trip or at a picnic with him. He was a regular fellow, if ever there was one.

My memory of John will always be his happy face

and manner, his hearty hand-clasp, his abounding praise, and his deep, sincere love for the Lord and His people.

When last I saw John, we went upon Garret Mountain which overlooks Paterson, our home town. One can see practically the entire city, besides New York, Newark, and nearer places. I thought by his silence that he was taking it all in, but his thoughts were far away. "Just think, Tom," he said at length, "that there are scores of cities in China, as large as this one, in which they do not have the Gospel."

That was the fact that loosened the hold of loved ones upon him and drew him away even from the work of the Star of Hope Mission. It was a hard parting, but it brought blessing to Paterson and other places where he spoke before leaving.

After a stay of six weeks in the Philadelphia home of the China Inland Mission, John was accepted for service on July 1, 1932. It was characteristic of his thoughtfulness and sincerity that, though invited to join the "Revelation Cruise" that summer, going with a large party of Christian friends to Bermuda and other places of interest, he declined, saying that it might be misunderstood in the light of the privations many missionaries were suffering, if he went on a cruise as luxurious as this one was to be. He crossed the continent by tourist car instead and sailed third class on the "Empress of Japan," with five other young men and two returning missionaries.

They were a united party and greatly enjoyed their visits to Honolulu and Japan, though the attitude of some of their fellow-travelers was none too friendly to missionaries. Yet those very people could not but be impressed by the manifest happiness of the little company.

It was amazing to see young fellows who sneered at the missionaries go ashore in Yokohama, and come back after their day of sin to tell us, one after another, how sick they were of it all, how they feared themselves and saw themselves slipping, and what a perfectly rotten time they had had; and still more amazing to have one of them say that he noticed that we missionary fellows seemed so free! And free we are! Not free to go into sin; even they didn't enjoy that; but free from sin with the remorse it brings, and able really to enjoy ourselves.

Yet there had been hours of painful suspense on that journey, if not of foreboding, to one of that little company. The letter John was eagerly expecting from Betty had not come. He had written, just as soon as he was accepted for China, asking the long-delayed question, and had looked for her reply before sailing. But the China mail had brought him nothing, not even a little friendly line. Was he so sure of his own love that he had counted too much upon hers? That was the question he could not get away from. And then another—was he really desiring only the will of God? Was he ready to face losing Betty out of his life?

At her up-river station, Betty also was tested with uncertainty. She had been designated to the city of Fowyang, in northern Anhwei, and longed to be there among the women. She had made unusual progress with the language, much of it coming back to her from early days, and it was hard to be kept away month after month from the work in which she was needed. But there was trouble in that part of the province. Mr. H. S. Ferguson, the senior missionary, had been captured by communist bandits and carried off into the mountains. His fate was uncertain,[1] and all the women missionaries had had to leave the district. When would they be able to go back? And what was happening to the Chinese Christians in their absence?

Dr. and Mrs. Scott, who had been on furlough, were returning to China that fall and requested that Betty might come to Shanghai to meet them. That she did; but their arrival was delayed, and she went back to her temporary station disappointed. Finally, when they did come, Betty was not very well, and the doctor in Shanghai found that her tonsils needed attention. He advised treatment that kept her at the coast a few weeks, and brought about most unexpected developments. For the "Empress of Japan" was rapidly nearing China, with John and his party on board.

The rest need hardly be told. What it meant to John to find that Betty was actually in Shanghai may be imagined. The joy was too deep for words; for nothing now prevented their open engagement. They had not brought it about. They had never imagined such a possibility. And everyone at headquarters seemed to share their happiness!

Traveling up the Yangtze a week later, when Betty was already on her way to Fowyang with returning missionaries, John wrote home to Paterson:

> I still cannot cease praising the Lord and wondering at His goodness in bringing Betty to Shanghai and keeping her there till I came! One of the boys from Australia asked me how we had "worked" it—and it was just blessed to realize that we hadn't worked it at all. It was unplanned and unexpected, as far as we were concerned. . . .
>
> Everybody about the Mission was so kind and sympathetic! One might have thought they would have their doubts about a new man coming out and getting engaged right off the bat! Several spoke of the coinci-

dence of Betty's being here just at the time. In fact, Mr. Lewis suggested that I ought to pay the doctor's bill, seeing I was getting the benefit of his treatment! And then, Mr. Gibb, the China Director, told me that he did not see any reason against our being married as soon as my year is up. So pray that the Lord will order this too as He wills.

Do you know, Tom [he added to a special friend], I almost shudder to think of the blessings I should have missed, had I not come out to China. All the way along, since I first started for the C.I.M home in Philadelphia, the way has been packed full of blessing. Even during the days on the steamer, when there was a good deal of uncertainty in my mind as to how things would turn out about Betty, the Lord did give such blessing to my soul! . . .

To me it has been a wonderful illustration of the fact that when we do "seek first" the kingdom of God, although our efforts may be blundering, He does unstintingly add the "all things."

---

[1]Mr. Henry S. Ferguson of Chengyangkwan, after thirty-seven years of devoted service, was taken by bandits on May 12, 1932. It is supposed that he was killed by his captors, but no details have ever come to light.

7

Faithful in Little

WHEN JOHN AND BETTY PARTED in Shanghai, it was not to meet again until the eve of their marriage a year later. John went up the Yangtze by river steamer to the city of Anking, there to join a group of twenty to thirty other young men in the language school of the mission. Betty traveled northward in the same great province of Anhwei, in the escort of Mr. and Mrs. Glittenberg, recently appointed to the work in Fowyang. The journey, first by train and then by bus, took several days and ended in a warm welcome from Mr. and Mrs. Hamilton, the only foreigners in the city. That was Betty's first experience of a more remote inland station.

> John is in southeastern Anhwei and I in the northwest. The great Yangtze is between our districts, and there are marked differences between the north and the south. They eat rice, for example, and we eat noodles. They have wet, green rice fields, and we have parched, dry wheat fields. We have the flattest country imaginable, while they have hills and valleys.

But in that dry, northern country there had been showers of spiritual blessing, as Betty soon discovered. In the province as a whole the work had been slow, without large ingatherings, until a few years previous when a springtide of divine grace visited that northern section. It was during the troublous years following 1925 that it began, and largely through the efforts of the local Christians. The general evacuation of 1927 had left the district without foreign missionaries, and the Chinese leaders were utterly cast upon God. In spite of much danger from communistic forces, they witnessed boldly for Christ, the Spirit of God working with them. So much was this the case that when Mr. Costerus and Mr. Hamilton returned, fearful of finding the Christians scattered and discouraged, they found instead a truly wonderful work of God throughout the Fowyang district.

In the city itself they met a Sunday congregation of 250, which they were told was the average attendance. A hearty Christian Endeavor meeting followed, and a baptismal service, when eleven men and fifteen women made public confession of Christ. At the Communion service afterward, seventy to eighty partook of the Lord's Supper, great joy overflowing their hearts. And those were people who had come through much persecution.

In an outstation thirty miles to the northwest, the believers were on fire for Christ. Persecution had put grit into them by the grace of God, and their testimony had been blessed to the conversion of many outsiders. Seventy-one men and women were examined and accepted for baptism. Their answers to the questions "were a splendid revelation," Mr. Costerus wrote, "of their knowledge of Scripture and the way of salvation."

A spirit of revival seemed to pervade the whole district. New groups of earnest Christians were meeting, week by week, to worship God. In one place a faithful widow had been the means of blessing and was keeping the converts together, some of them already taking the lead in the Sunday services. But the need of teaching among the young believers was very pressing. Of two villages where there were fairly large groups, Mr. Costerus wrote:

> None of them know much of the Gospel. About all they can do, when they come together, is to sing and pray. But the Lord is working among them. They are spoken of as "wild sheep" at present, because there is nobody to care for them.

The thankfulness of the missionaries at being able to return to the district may be imagined, and when Mr. and Mrs. Hamilton had to leave on furlough, the Glittenbergs were appointed to take their place. Miss Nancy Rodgers remained on in charge of the girls' school in Fowyang and much other work, and gave the warmest welcome to Betty Scott and her companion Katie Dodd.

The autumn conference was wonderful that year as hundreds of Christians gathered in Fowyang. They came from all parts of the district, full of expectation of blessing. Betty wrote,

> We were very glad to have Miss Rodgers back again, and the joy of the Chinese was unbounded. She brought a Miss Chiang from Süancheng with her, who took part in the autumn meetings. These were certainly well attended. There must have been eight hundred present, for the church was tightly packed. Many of the Christians came from country places.

Eighty-two were baptized that autumn, including one old gentleman more than eighty years of age, of whom Mrs. Glittenberg wrote:

> When he returned home after the baptismal service, his wayward son, who had given him much concern,

said to his surprise: "It will never do for the two of us to live in the same house now!" He thought that he was too deep in sin to be saved. But the father persuaded him to agree that he could at least be prayed for. Some of the elders of the church came in answer to their request. They talked and prayed with the young man, and he was gloriously saved.

It was not easy to go on with language study in the midst of such opportunities throughout the district. Betty and Miss Dodd were able to do some visiting in the city, however, and even before the conference had taken one week for an evangelistic journey. Of that new experience she wrote to her young brother:

> Anhwei is the flattest country you ever saw in your life. It's almost like the ocean when very calm, with only here and there a bunch of trees and houses which can't be seen far off, as the houses are mud and the trees dusty, like everything else. Sometimes, the first we saw of a homestead was the bunch of brilliant red peppers, hanging up to dry against a wall. These and the persimmon trees, which have a glorious way of turning color so that every leaf is a different hue, ranging from all oranges and reds to green, were almost the only bits of live color that we saw all day. Everywhere the people were harvesting pinky-gray sweet potatoes, out of what looked like piles of dry dust. Whenever a little donkey trotted by, it raised a cloud of dust that could be seen for miles. Sometimes we were beside the river, which was almost blue, and had cut deep banks for itself out of dry cliffs.
>
> Our ricksha men went along at the slowest walk. The road was bumpy and the tires were not balloon, or new. Most of them were wrapped around with swaddling bands, and the men anxiously stopped to pick burrs off them, for fear of more punctures.
>
> About 2:30 we stopped for dinner. No, it wasn't a rest

station, and there wasn't a sign of gas anywhere. It was a market town, and every man, woman, and child for miles around was there with their produce, trying to see who could collect most flies on them and their food. When the flies saw us, they were tickled pink and made for us! So did the people. We retired into a little inner room of a mud house (the inn) and there the people rushed us as though we were a couple of footballs. The landlady shoved them out bodily, explaining in loud tones that we were only human beings like themselves. But they, good-naturedly, sneaked in anyway, until they were three deep all around us.

The landlady was evidently kind as well as vigorous. Determined to secure a measure of privacy for her guests, she made an excuse to take them to a back courtyard and hurried them into another little room.

Firmly closing the door, she left us to our meal with chopsticks in almost total darkness, not even able to see whether we were eating any of the flies! Such of the crowd as were already in before the door was shut, gleamed at us with shining eyes. They had a lovely show—the big excitement of their lives! All this time we had been giving out tracts as well as we could, our Bible-woman doing most of the talking.

Well, that night we stopped at another village, where there were some Christians and a place of worship. These dear people were no cleaner than anybody else, but they were awfully friendly and nice. They brought us hot water and boiled peanuts and all kinds of things. We slept in a loft over the little chapel. The rats bothered Katie, so she hauled her bedding down the ladder and slept on some benches. I stayed up above, but got a raft of smaller things than rats—ai-yah!

The next day we reached Yingshan, a rather large city. The wall could be seen for miles across the plain. No missionary, as far as we know, has ever lived there. Our premises are back from the main streets and have the loveliest, round, moon gate you ever saw, leading to the inner courtyard. The evangelist who occupies them now with his family, had very Chinesey turnips and shrimps drying in the sun all over the place, with many flies to every shrimp.

That outstation was not in the part of the district where there had been most blessing, and it was hoped that Betty and Miss Dodd would go and live there before long to care for the women and children. Betty rejoiced at the prospect.

This place is the most promising I can imagine for such work. Little has been done among the women, and there are quite a few who have heard something of the Gospel and are eager to learn to read and study the Bible. Somehow or other, their hearts have been prepared. It is the same with the children. Schoolboys and girls, as well as those who cannot read, just beamed at the idea that we should teach them. They swarmed in all the time we were there, and every verse or Bible chorus that we knew they were eager to learn. They would repeat them over hundreds of times to make sure that they had really got them. . . .

Some among them were the most precious little children you ever saw — really lovable, unspoiled ones, whose eyes just shone, and who crowded round us and repeated every word we said, every verse and chorus, line by line, for hours. There was no such thing as rushing in late for Sunday school, and rushing home again right afterward. They did go home for meals, but not all at the same time! There were three services on Sunday, led by the evangelist, and a special children's meeting in the afternoon, so the place was packed all day long. They weren't fresh and cheeky either; they were simply interested and thrilled. We gave them tracts, and Miss Liu nearly talked her head off, preaching to group after group of women. All of them wanted us to come back later and live in the city, and teach them the Bible.

It was tiring work, and the girls were unused to such surroundings. Language, food, crowds — all were strange; but how glad they were to be there! To her fiancé at Anking Betty wrote:

O John, how the people streamed in, yesterday, after our arrival! They were in the chapel, which is largely open, in the courtyard, in our room — everywhere! And there were the loveliest young girls, besides crowds of women, students, and children. We gave out many tracts, and the Bible-woman was talking almost every minute. Katie and I attempted a few words, here and there. I counted fifty or sixty listening at one time, and they kept coming and going. We invited them all back for Sunday, to the preaching services. How we long to start Bible classes for these educated girls, and other meetings for the women and children!

This morning the evangelist took us on a flying visit to each of the homes where there are Christians and inquirers, and there is surely lots of work to be done! Imagine — no missionary, man or woman, has ever lived here, and I don't think any white woman has ever been here before, except Mrs. Ferguson. It is a large walled city too.

John was naturally anxious for Betty's safety in a district that was not free from bandits, especially after a sad experience that immediately followed Betty's journey. Little Lois, the youngest of the Glittenberg children, a lovely baby with golden curls all over her head, was taken ill with dysentery. Betty was devoted to the family and felt deeply for Mrs. Glittenberg when, as the only hope of saving the child's life, she set out to take her by bus to the nearest hospital, a long day's journey. Sad to say, the bus was stopped by bandit soldiers who ordered all the passengers out and took possession of their baggage. In vain Mrs. Glittenberg pleaded for the little bag which contained the baby's medicine and a few other necessities. The bandits concluded that the bag must be especially valuable, since the mother was so concerned about it and refused to give it up. There was a long delay before rickshas could be found to take the travelers on to their destination. Happily Mrs. Glittenberg had money sewed up in her clothing and was able to pay her way, but the long exposure cost the precious little life. Baby Lois died of dysentery in the hospital in Hwaiyüan. Telling of that sorrow and the beautiful spirit in which the parents took it, Betty wrote a few days later:

> Here in this work, you just have to trust everything to God, including your children, and know that He will do exactly what is best, and according to His will.

That was in November, only a few weeks after Betty's arrival with the Glittenbergs in Fowyang, and before the close of the year they had another trying experience, that time with soldiers. Betty's letter about it was written to John at Anking:

December 11, 1932

Today I did not go to church, and about noon went over to the Glittenbergs to dinner. Milton has been sick since the baby died, and now it looks as if it may be measles. Mrs. Glittenberg was with him, and all the others were at church, except the cook who had returned early to release the old gateman. It was 2 P.M. and church was not over, when a couple of soldiers marched in and sat down to stay. Apparently the cook opposed them, for they hit him, and he rushed off to the church compound to get the gateman and Mr. Wang, the teacher of the girl's school. Meanwhile I went out and spoke to the soldiers, explaining that there was only a girls' school here, the missionary's residence, and a few rooms occupied by other people (meaning that there would be no room to entertain them and their company). Well, by the time the cook had brought Mr. Wang and the gateman back, it was evident that the soldiers meant to stay, so I went in and told Mrs. Glittenberg. Then church was dismissed and all the girls came home. You can imagine the situation when, before long, there were two companies of men (about sixty soldiers) downstairs in the girls' school, and all the desks and tables out in the courtyard.

It is most improper, of course, for soldiers to take possession of any part of a girls' school building that way, even though Nancy Rodgers and the girls stayed upstairs, and they would certainly proceed to wander all over the compound and our house too. Mr. Glittenberg had gone down to Shanghai, to bring the older children back for the Christmas holidays, and the pastor was away on a preaching tour, so the evangelist, Mr. Ho, who had just brought the tent back from some good meetings, politely but firmly tried to explain matters.

About that time, we decided that I had better go over to the church compound to see how Katie's and my place was faring, since soldiers were evidently quartering all over. As I returned, finding everything quiet over there, I passed Mr. Ho near the yamen (residence of the official in charge of the district) and, bless his heart! he went to find the real "big bug," whom he actually met just outside the door. The chief was very friendly, and when he heard that it was a Christian girls' school, he said at once that it was not suitable that his men should remain there. They should be out, he promised, before dark.

But the men were very much in occupation by that time, and were beginning to peer around into our kitchen and Nancy's rooms in the second story of the school. We were glad to hear Mr. Ho's report, but kept right on praying, because people can change their minds or find excuses, if they wish to do so. However, as we were praying —my, it was wonderful!—we heard a sharp whistle and some commands being given, and before we could get out to see, the men were lining up at attention, in a long double file stretching from our door almost to the front gate. Out they marched in good order, and the whole place was clear and quiet before dark. Mr. Ho, teacher Wang, the gateman, the carpenter, the little goat boy, the cook, the schoolgirls and we ourselves went grinning around in a joyful sort of daze, praising the mercy of God, as you may believe, again and again.

Commenting on those happenings in a letter to his parents John said:

I was specially glad to see the cool way in which Betty was taking it all. I do thank God for her. But the above will help you to pray more understandingly for her—for us both when we get out into the work. One never knows what one may run into. But we do know that the Lord Jehovah reigns. Above all, don't let anything worry you about us.

He then quoted a poem that had just reached him, written about the death of a missionary at the hands of bandit soldiers. Gun in hand, they asked him if he was afraid. "No," he replied, "if you shoot, I go straight to Heaven!"[1] John continued,

And so we can praise God that, for us, everything is well. If we should go on before, it is only the quicker to enjoy the bliss of the Saviour's presence, the sooner to be released from the fight against sin and Satan. Meanwhile we can continue to praise Him from whom all blessings flow.

In his own work at Anking, John was very conscious of help in answer to prayer. He was finding the language difficult, but his letters were full of good cheer and confidence in God. The faithfulness in little things that had characterized him as a boy at school was still more manifest now—in his use of his time and steady application to the task in hand. He was improving, too, in health, through keeping early hours and taking exercise. The students at Anking were not able to go out much, lest the appearance of so many young men should cause excitement in the city; but they made up for lack of walking exercise by strenuous open-air sports in their own compound. Passing his language tests after the first few months was a great experience to John.

Hurrah! This morning I finished the last of the three language exams. I have taken one a day for three days . . . and praise the Lord for His help, of which I have been very conscious. . . . On Wednesday I take my oral, reading from selected passages and holding a conversation with the pastor, rather than with one of our regular teachers. Then on Saturday I am to lead morning worship in Chinese, the subject for the day being John 5:15-23. I am glad it is not too abstruse a passage.

March 25, 1932

When we first came out, and read what Hudson Taylor said about men preaching in Chinese six months after beginning to study, we smiled. But here it is—just one day more than five months, and I have actually taken morning prayers! Praise the Lord!

I suppose it is because I have already shaken in my shoes so many times at street corners all over Paterson, that I'm not too badly affected that way now. . . . It was certainly blessed to realize that I could say a bit and get over some ideas which were apparently understood. Not being able to pray in Chinese as yet, I asked the pastor to do so, and from the way he went over all the points of the message it was evident that he had taken it in, even if he was repeating it for the benefit of those who may not have understood.

The general director of the mission was expected at Anking by that time to go into the important matter of designations, and there was not a little speculation among the students as to where each one would be sent. As the mission carries on its work in fifteen provinces of China proper, as well as in its outlying dependencies, the field is a wide one, and the needs of very different kinds of work have to be considered. Much prayer had been made about the matter all through the winter, and the young men had learned enough about the country to be taken into consultation. Mr. Hoste arrived on a Monday and began his interviews the same day. John wrote,

> I didn't come on till the afternoon of Tuesday. Mr. Hoste had caught a bit of a cold and had to stay in bed that day. . . . I don't think I'll ever forget the time I had with him alone.
>
> When you see Mr. Hoste under ordinary circumstances, his massive head, perfectly erect figure and pointed beard proclaim the fact that he was formerly an army officer. But it is different when you see him in bed, propped up with pillows. There wasn't a suggestion of the officer about him. He looked more like a tired patriarch, ready to lay his burdens down. He just made me think of Jacob, leaning on his staff, blessing his sons.
>
> I was only with him a few minutes, when he began to pray. He asked the Lord to bless me and to bless Betty — gladdening my heart, by the way — and went on to pray for the Mission, the native church, other missions and so on, for fifteen or twenty minutes. I could not help feeling that this was not so much just a bowing of the head to ask the Lord to bless our deliberations, but that, when he began to pray, he forgot that I had

come to be designated and was on his most important work, that of intercession.

Then he went on to give me helpful advice on all lines, not in a haughty tone, but in a truly humble way. . . . Finally, after I had been an hour with him, he came round to the designation. The outcome is that I am to go to Süancheng for further study and a start in the work with Mr. and Mrs. Birch, from North America. Then it is intended that we open a new station in a city called Tsingteh. So, if I'm not out in Sinkiang, it looks as if it will still be our privilege to occupy new territory for the Lord. . . .

Not knowing Süancheng, I cannot write much about it, except to say that there is evidently a prosperous church there. It is in mountainous country in the south of this province, which is said to be very beautiful.

Then came farewells at the language school and the breaking up of the first happy associations in China.

I shall ever thank God for my acquaintance with John [wrote one of his fellow students]. He was the most spiritual fellow in Anking; it was a joy to talk or work with him. He always seemed to be above difficulties and worries, for he turned them over to God, and his example encouraged several (I know it did me) to be more diligent in prayer.

John was the backbone, humanly speaking, of the spiritual life at Anking that winter [said another who had traveled with him from America]. He seemed to know Christ more intimately, more practically than the rest of us. When I was discouraged, he helped me to find the joy of the Lord. Some months after we had left Anking, he wrote me a letter of sympathetic reproof for certain things, a letter which I treasure and will often reread with profit. I never, before or since, received a reproof more truly in the spirit of Galatians 6:1, and I praise God for it. John's spirituality was radiant and

contagious. He seemed to be always in touch with the
source of power, even our Lord Himself.

¹This poem is given in full on page 117. It concerns the noble steadfastness of the Rev. J. W. Vinson, martyred in North China, and was written
by another China missionary, the Rev. E. H. Hamilton. For letters from the
sons of Mr. Vinson, see page 135. This poem meant much to John. He
received it from Dr. C. E. Scott.

8

Faithful Also in Much

IT WAS ONE of Mr. Hudson Taylor's helpful sayings that "a little thing is a little thing, but *faithfulness* in a little thing is a great thing." To John and Betty, who had been faithful above all in their hidden walk with God, was now to be entrusted the great riches of a perfect love in married life and a wide field of service.

But before taking up his new responsibilities John had the summer for study, and instead of accepting an invitation to the shore to escape the great heat, he chose to spend it alone in his new district among the Chinese. Süancheng, the central station, was in the charge of Mr. George A. Birch, who was glad to welcome him as a fellow worker.

How clearly I remember the day John arrived at Süancheng. I met him at the launch. He was six feet two, every inch a man. His hearty grip and bright smile clinched our friendship at once. As we proceeded in the sampan (little boat, for shallow water) the conversation soon turned to the things of God, for John lived with God and loved to talk of the things that were filling his heart.

On our first itineration together we had to walk all one day in the rain and mud, but John's ardor was in no way dampened. That trip, and all our trips together, were a blessing to me, for John's mind was a mine of wealth in the knowledge of God. He truly was mighty in the Scriptures, full of zeal to make Christ known, and full of love to the lost souls around him.

John was very quick to see the hand of God in everything. One day he was "all in" from a heavy cold and tired from a long walk. We felt the need of some green vegetables with our food, but saw no possibility of getting any. At noon we stopped to preach the Gospel in a village, and without any word from us the woman at the door of whose tea shop we were preaching, and who knew our Chinese companion, prepared a good meal for us. There were six or eight different kinds of vegetables, most of them nicely salted, for they were out of season at the time. What a surprise! John exclaimed, "Can God furnish a table in the wilderness?" How often he would say, "My heavenly Father knows"!

Mr. and Mrs. Birch were going to the hills that summer for much needed change, so that from the middle of June John was left alone in charge. And he had only been eight months in China.

He made marvelous progress with the language and got very close to the people. During that time he carried on regular meetings for the children, and one Sunday even led the church service, preaching a sermon in Chinese.

John's own letters give glimpses of the inward side of these experiences that were not all easy.

Well, I am all alone now [he wrote in July]. But it's not half as bad as it sounds, and a good home letter did a lot to remind me of my great privilege one day when I was a bit tinged with blue. . . .

What I have been enjoying most is to get out distributing a few tracts, and having a chance to talk with people. Last night I stopped in two shops where men asked me to sit down a bit, and had a good talk with them about the Gospel, though my vocabulary is still so painfully limited.

Here's telling you that these last weeks have been about the most blessed I have ever known. People laugh at my Chinese! It's a fright to try to get all they say to me, and I am only partly successful in getting my ideas across. The goat may die, thieves may come in and turn the compound into a place for a midnight manhunt, there may be plenty of interruptions and difficulties of one kind and another, but through it all has been the steady consciousness of the Lord's presence. . . .

I've had quite a number of young students coming lately. Pray that I may be able to give them the Gospel clearly. I usually have a good Scripture tract handy, which I give to one of them and ask him to read it for us. Then a few words of explanation, and so forth. As yet I can't do what I should like to —ask questions to bring out what they think or believe, and then try to give them something really to fit their needs. My words are still too few, and I can only understand a fraction of what they say. Many of them, too, are probably more interested in just seeing the foreigner, and hearing the phonograph or organ. So there it is! But they do get some Gospel truth from me, and more in a tract or Scripture portion.

Tired after long days of study in the heat, he found refreshment in the beauty of nature around him.

Many a night I go outside the city gate, or up on the wall, and just stand and watch the clouds. It's like a benediction and a choir singing anthems and a wonderful sermon all rolled into one. So you see I am not without my enjoyments. About ten miles on either side of us are hills and mountains, and the sunsets are just grand.

He was getting up early, and working in the garden

for an hour every morning before breakfast, "for exercise and delight at the same time," as he put it. So that he kept in health and got through his second section of language study before the time came to go northward for his bride. In August he wrote about putting up sixty quarts of preserves and jams for the absent housemother, commenting, "Didn't think that has anything to do with missionary work, but it seems to!"

Had a great day with a very nice young fellow this morning. He seemed really interested and I was able to pray with him. Then in the afternoon four more students dropped in. A small group have been coming more or less regularly, and we have gone through John's Gospel, chapter by chapter. . . . Pray much for these young fellows.

And the children were a great joy. John was making use of Scripture choruses put to Chinese music. He wrote in August:

The children in our afternoon and Sunday meetings sing them like anything. I don't think you could sit in this room for an hour, except at night, without hearing some little kid going off on a Scripture song at full tilt at the top of his lungs. . . . The other morning, quite early, I heard one little girl singing joyfully, "Yes, Jesus loves me, the Bible tells me so." Well, it really thrilled me! For I knew that people all about her, to whom I can talk so little, were getting the Gospel, because she was singing to them.

After almost a year of steady grind at the language, he found it wonderfully refreshing to be traveling by steamer and train up to Dr. and Mrs. Scott's home in Tsinan. He wrote to his family:

I feel like taking a couple of days off just to praise the Lord:

1. Because I'm saved and in the Lord's service.
2. For excellent health, despite the hottest summer known here in years.
3. For more freedom in the language.
4. That I shall soon be returning, D.V., with my *wife* —I like that phrase too!

The warmth of his welcome in Tsinan may be judged from a letter of Betty's, written some months previously to Mr. Harry Stam, the brother in Africa:

> It is good that John has a real sense of humor. He is such an easy person to get along with! You should hear Mother rave about him. Even if I hadn't wanted him, Mother would have stuck to him through thick and thin and given me no peace until I gave in! Mother just took to him from the very first. Daddy doesn't say so much, but he feels pretty good about it too. They are making plans for the wedding at a great rate, and Daddy seems to be thinking about all the details.

It was toward the end of October that the bridal party gathered at Tsinan. Betty had been home a month or more, after an absence of ten years, and John had had some quiet days with her before the bridesmaids and best man arrived. These were fellow workers of the China Inland Mission, Katherine Dodd and Nancy Rodgers from Fowyang, and Percy Bromley, who had been with John in the language school. The maid of honor was Betty's roommate and chief friend of Wilson College days, Marguerite Luce, a missionary nurse working in the Presbyterian hospital at Chefoo.

> When the morning of October 25 dawned [wrote the bride's mother] we were all filled with thankfulness that God had so wonderfully answered our prayers about the weather. It was a perfect day, not a cloud in the sky all the day long, also without wind or dust, and warmer than it had been for several days past. We could

go ahead with our plans for converting our tennis court, east of the house, into an open-air chapel.

The court easily lends itself to a delightful transformation. It runs north and south, and on three sides is lined with trees and shrubbery. On the fourth side, the south wall is a solid mass of ivy, the leaves of which were just turning red and gold. From the seats, facing south, guests could see over the wall the top of a range of hills near the city. . . . Long benches with backs, brought over from the compound church, were arranged to leave a wide aisle down the center and an open space at the south end for the ceremony. This was banked in with palms and ferns and flowering plants. . . . Rugs covered the cement floor there, and down the central aisle. . . .

The bridegroom and best man with the officiating clergyman, our next door neighbor, the Rev. Reuben A. Torrey,[1] approached by a path through the garden from the west side. The bridesmaids wearing lavender silk and carrying bouquets of yellow chrysanthemums and asparagus fern, tied with wide yellow ribbons, came slowly down the central aisle, followed by the maid of honor in a dress of the same princess style of lavender.

The bride, on the arm of her father, wore a simple gown of white silk crepe, with wide sleeves and a long skirt. At the open neck was Brussels lace, like the lace across the front of her cap-fitted veil. We all thought she looked specially lovely, as she moved with ease and grace in our midst. On her lips was a sweet, happy smile, while she kept her eyes steadily on the face of the bridegroom. . . . And he, waiting at the altar, had eyes for her alone.

We have witnessed many Chinese weddings, even among Christians, when the bride never once glanced up into the face of the bridegroom, keeping her head bowed as if in sorrow and trepidation, and could not but feel that the willing, trustful attitude in this case made a deep impression on our Chinese friends, espe-

90

cially the students.[2]

Mr. Torrey in his ministerial robes added dignity to the simple, impressive service. Everyone seemed to feel a reverence and sacred joy in witnessing the union of two such devoted, consecrated young lives. Many of the guests, both Chinese and foreigners, spoke afterward of the helpfulness of the service to them personally.

A perfect day came to a close when, after the bridal party had dined together and had evening worship with beautiful hymns, John and Betty left for Tsingtao, the home of her childhood. John wrote on October 27:

> This letter is from your newly married couple at Tsingtao. Oh, the Lord has been so good in all the arrangements that we are just praising Him all along the way! We are having a most blessed time together, and there is so much to tell you that I am going to see if I cannot lay violent hands on some typewriter around here, before our blessings pile up so high that I may forget some of them.
>
> Just to show you how wondrously happy the Lord has made us, I must tell you of a remark Betty made yesterday. We were speaking of one poor fellow all alone here in China, and she exclaimed so naturally, "John dear, don't you wish all our single friends would get married!"
>
> I am sure none of the boys [his brothers] has had so lovely a honeymoon as Betty and I are having—perfect fall weather with gorgeous foliage and this seaside mountain place, seemingly all to ourselves! An architect friend of Dr. Scott's took us up to his cottage in the mountains about two hours from here. We stayed the night. All around were great rocky peaks, it was just grand! The next morning, Betty and I walked up one valley toward a waterfall. It was lovely, with clear crystal pools and rocks on all sides. We never saw a single European all the way, and only a couple of Chinese. It was so deserted that we could sing and yodel freely as

we went along. . . . Truly our God seems to go out of His way to make His children happy.

But married life like theirs has a way of getting better and better all along. They may have felt that nothing could ever be quite so perfect as those two weeks at Tsingtao, but when they got back to Süancheng and settled down in their own little home for a winter of work and study, it was even more wonderful.

John is out for the week end [Betty wrote early in December], and next week end he and I are planning to visit another outstation, where he is to lead his first Communion Service in Chinese. That will be my first trip in this part of the country. We have had the tailor and his men busy for some days, and both of us are now fixed up with Chinese garments. You ought to see John in his fur-lined gown! He looks taller than ever. And watch him gather his arms up under the skirts in the back, when he is going downstairs, for all the world like an old Chinese gentleman!

While living in their own quarters on the mission compound, the young couple took their meals with Mr. and Mrs. Birch, to save double housekeeping. But many a quiet evening was spent by their own fireside (or stove), John with his books at one end of the table and Betty at the other. She was preparing for the last of her examinations in the language, which she took a few months later, thus completing within three years the course of study required for women workers of the mission. But though eager to get on with the language, they did not neglect opportunities of getting out with Chinese fellow workers.

I do thank the Lord for bringing me to this station [John had written on his first arrival at Süancheng], for there are many fine Christians here, and it is a good place to work out from.

It was with Song, the tailor, one of these voluntary workers, that John and Betty made their first trip together to an outstation. Four hours' walk, including many conversations by the wayside, brought them to Swenchiapu, where they were hospitably welcomed by Pao, the silversmith. Of these friends John wrote:

> Both Song and Pao Lao-pan, at whose home we stayed, are real Christians and a great blessing in the work. Song, especially, gives whole weeks of his time to going out over the country preaching. He gets nothing for it, but praises God for the opportunity of making known the Gospel. It is good to hear him tell how at one time he was afraid to leave his business and go off in this way, but now that he observes Sunday and has his apprentices do so too, the Lord has given him honest men, so that he can be free.[3] I wish you could see that man's face, just smiling out the joy and thankfulness he has in the Lord!

Mr. Pao too had had encouraging experiences in the difficult matter of keeping Sunday. He had been burdened with a debt of seven hundred dollars and felt that to be a sufficient excuse for working on the Lord's Day. How could he hope to pay even the exorbitant interest (three per cent a month) unless he kept his shop open seven days a week, like everyone else! But a visit from Mr. Birch set him thinking. The missionary had shown him some wonderful promises from the Bible, God's own promises to those who please Him by keeping His commandments. Faith was strengthened, and Pao determined, at any cost, to close his business on Sunday.

Right across the street was another silversmith who hoped to profit by what he considered Pao's foolishness, and openly reviled him for having "eaten of the foreigner's religion." But Pao was quiet and patient,

93

and his business did not suffer. Just then gold began to be in demand. Pao kept in touch with the exchange in other places, and was able to make considerable profits, to the envy of his rival. Before long the entire debt was cleared away. A little later, strange to say, fire swept that part of the city. The houses opposite Mr. Pao's were completely destroyed. The flames came right up to his premises. His roof, even, was slightly damaged. But, suddenly, as he was crying to God for protection, the wind changed. His whole place was saved, as by a miracle. No wonder he loved to tell of the power and watchful care of his heavenly Father.

We had a happy time with Mr. Pao. On Saturday we went round giving out tracts and talking with people in their homes, and at night had a crowded meeting. But Sunday was the great day. In the morning there was a meeting for worship, after which we observed the Lord's Supper. Truly the Lord blessed us richly! In the afternoon we first had an hour in the street chapel, then went out for two big open-air meetings, and at night there was again a large, attentive audience in the street chapel. . . .

We were specially happy on the trip back. Betty had been able to go out with Mrs. Pao, and also to help at the open-air meetings and with the children, so our hearts were already full of praise. But Monday brought further opportunities. It took about six hours to walk the ten miles home, stopping every now and then with groups along the way. It was really delightful! At one town where we stayed for lunch, we had a good open-air meeting. We finally arrived at Süancheng with every tract given out and every Gospel sold, and with a big blessing in our own souls.

During Chinese New Year, when folks are free to enjoy the one annual holiday, Betty was able to take a longer trip with John to the district that was to be their special parish. Lying some sixty miles southwest of Süancheng, it proved to be a beautiful, mountainous region, with many towns and villages along the fertile valleys. As that was the district in which their brief missionary service was soon to be consummated, the visit in February, 1934, is of special and pathetic interest. Their center was to be the little city of Tsingteh, where they stayed a week with Mr. and Mrs. S. J. Warren, who were leaving shortly for furlough. Formerly a wealthy city, it had been a favorite residence of noble families in attendance on the emperor, but all that glory had long gone by. The T'ai-ping Rebellion, which almost depopulated the district in the early part of the last century, had left Tsingteh largely in ruins. Betty wrote:

Our premises here are thoroughly Chinesey, but big and roomy. . . . There is not much yet in the way of Christian life, but there are one or two bright spots, and God is our hope anyway, or we would never attempt the work. . . . Ancestral halls abound, and ancestral worship with the strong clan system will form our greatest hindrance —excepting always our own selves.

We enjoy the scenery all about us here very much, only it looks like another case of "every prospect pleases, and only man is vile." . . . The people live in greater comfort, compared with other places, eat better food and probably are more self-satisfied. Many have old mansions, full of spacious halls, with wonderful carved beams and woodwork. Even in the inns, coming down, we rarely encountered fleas or allied pests, a condition undreamed of in the north. There are lovely stone bridges over clear-flowing streams. The rice fields everywhere are most picturesque. So are the high, grass-covered mountains and the blue, misty peaks beyond.

Do pray about the beginning of work here. We have a fine street chapel at the front of our premises and a comfortable place at the rear, made out of one of the old Chinese houses, now screened and fixed up.

One of the bright spots Betty referred to was the outstation at Miaosheo, ten miles across the mountains, or at any rate, one family of Christians there who welcomed the young missionaries with every possible kindness. Miaosheo and the evangelist Lo, of whom John wrote in the following letter, are names that will go down in the annals of Christian heroism for all time to come:

Saturday morning we went to Miaosheo where the evangelist, Mr. Lo, with whom I am to be working, will have his home. The trip was only a short one, about thirty-five *li*, but beautiful beyond words — part of the time down a long valley that winds in and out among tree-covered hills. The walking was good, for it was over stone-covered roads a large part of the way. . . . Most of the Miaosheo Christians live out in the country, and right now the church certainly needs to be revived. Pray for them and for Mr. Lo, who will act as their pastor when he is at home.

At Miaosheo we stayed in the home of Mr. Wang, who was the first Christian in these parts. Years ago one of our present directors and his wife were passing through this district, and reaching Miaosheo about nightfall were looking round for a place to stay in. While Mrs. Gibb was still in her sedan chair, Mr. Gibb began to preach on the street. Mrs. Wang was one of those who heard. She ran to fetch her husband, and both of them received the truth, though it was the first time they had ever heard it. They invited Mr. and Mrs. Gibb to their home that night. Later, when Mrs. Wang was asked if she believed the Gospel, "How could one help believing," was her answer, "when told of such wonderful love?"

Sunday in Miaosheo was a good day, the Christians gathering with interest to meet the new missionaries. Gladly would John and Betty have stayed with them, but they had several other places to visit before returning to Süancheng. The journey occupied twenty-four days in all, and took them over a high mountain pass into the province of Chekiang, a corner of which lay in their field.

This trip was getting right down into the thick of the mountains. The valleys were much narrower and passes higher to climb. Most of the way was good stone road. About noon it rained, so that we made about half our journey in a downpour. Still it was beautiful, for the path led in and out along the mountain curves, high above the gushing brook at the bottom, with little thatched homes and corn clearings still higher above us. We had a good meeting that night in the town of Chiki.

Next day we went on to the home of our Pastor Cheng's people, over in Chekiang. . . . There were about eighteen church members there, and it was good to hear them sing the hymns to their own tunes. In the afternoon we had a baptismal service which the pastor conducted. It was interesting to meet his old father.

Years ago a peddler had passed through that region and old Mr. Cheng, then a schoolteacher, had bought one of the gospels bound up with the book of Acts. Many an hour he spent carefully reading the little book, until he was convinced that it was a message from the true God. The peddler came again some time later, and Mr. Cheng eagerly asked him if there was not more of that story. From his reading he had discovered that he had only part of a larger book. Yes, the peddler said, he would bring him the rest. And so Mr. Cheng came into possession of the whole Bible. What a treasure to have found its way into those remote valleys!

After many experiences of persecution and wonderful answers to prayer, the old man was still standing firm in the faith, and his testimony had led not a few others to Christ.

> It was a joy to see him in the meetings — arrayed in a foreign style overcoat with great wide sleeves, a battered foreign hat, and rimless glasses, his head thrown back, singing with all his might! Why look at a book? He seemed to know all the hymns by heart!

A perilous journey over high mountain passes had to be negotiated on leaving the village. The climb up was stiff, and Betty walked all the way, but the path down on the other side was still more precipitous. At first she preferred to clamber down on foot, rather than to risk sliding out of the chair, but as the descent was about two miles she was finally persuaded to ride.

> Believe me, I prayed [wrote John, who was walking behind]. In places where the path doubled back on itself, the front bearer would be down ever so far, and the back one up, with Betty in the chair hanging over the abyss below! I walked close back of the rear man, and once threw away my stick and grabbed the poles when he slipped a bit. I surely breathed a sigh of relief when we reached the bottom! It was a long hard day, from 7:30 A.M. to 7 P.M.

The next day made up for weariness, however, when they reached the river and were able to hire a boat for Süancheng. John added:

> Talk about solid comfort — the boat boards were solid enough, but with our bedding we were able to sleep and read in comfort until we arrived home that night.
>
> Do praise the Lord for keeping us in good health and spirits, and for the work He has given us to do. It is sobering to think that under God we are responsible to

98

give the Gospel to such a big slice of our Anhwei province with a corner of Chekiang thrown in. The valleys just teem with villages. Oh, that the Lord might have an assembly of true worshipers in each one!

Betty was not able to travel much after that on account of new hopes that were making the future look very bright.

Of Betty and John's last year I have two specially vivid impressions [wrote her sister, Mrs. Mahy]. One is the long walking and preaching trip they took among the mountains. . . . They were wonderfully happy and exhilarated over it and over doing it together, though Daddy and Mother were concerned, fearing the trip would be too much for her. The other impression is the anticipation and preparation for that little one. I realized during the months before she came that Betty was making more loving and careful preparation for her than I had over both of mine put together. She and John discussed many possible names for the baby, and their letters were crammed full of their love for her. . . . I devoured those letters even more eagerly, I think, than the ones about their evangelistic journeys.

[1] Son of Dr. R. A. Torrey, the well-known evangelist.

[2] Of the two hundred guests present, about one hundred forty were Chinese Christians.

[3] Mr. Song closes his shop on Sundays, paying his five assistants the same as ever, and bringing them to church with him. Of course his competitors think it is a pure loss, but Song knows better and praises the Lord that his business prospers.

9

Little Helen Priscilla

IT WAS IN THE BEAUTIFUL Methodist hospital at Wuhu, over-looking far reaches of the Yangtze, that little Helen Priscilla made her appearance on September 11, 1934. She was a lovely baby from the first. Her father, who had been warned not to expect too much of a newborn infant, wrote in delighted surprise:

> But you should see our daughter! She really is the cutest little thing . . . and would do for any baby show, as far as good looks is concerned, right now.

Betty's first letter to the home folks in Paterson was written a few weeks later:

> The baby looks like John, nearly everybody says. She has his mouth and chin. Her eyes are a deep blue and very big, and her face is so sweet and round! She has a lot of dark hair that is actually curly when damp. We cannot say she never cries . . . but during the night she sleeps soundly from 10 P.M. to 6 A.M. —and most of the time from 6 A.M. to 10 P.M.

When little Helen was three weeks old, she had a visit from her grandmother who came all the way from Tsinan to welcome her arrival. Mrs. Scott stayed until Betty

101

was quite herself again and able to take care of the little one. With all the solicitude of a young mother, she wrote on being left in charge:

Baby weighs 9 pounds and 3 ounces today. It is a real joy to take care of her. I am always wondering if she is too warm or too cold, and running around to feel her hands and feet. She won't keep her arms under the covers, so I slip on an extra knitted jacket, backside front. Last evening she howled and kicked so hard that I am afraid it was temper. For the minute anyone picks her up she is as placid and serene as can be, with a slightly reproachful expression, as much as to say, "Why didn't you come sooner?" So we shall have to be very strict with her!

By that time John was back in the Tsingteh district.

I knew he was champing his bit to go and see the Christians, to find out about conditions and to go evangelizing during this beautiful fall weather.

It was a joy to be with the Wangs again at Miaosheo, though he found that the long, hot summer had resulted in widespread destruction of the crops. Mrs. Wang's welcome was as loving as ever. A glimpse into this home is afforded in one of John's earlier letters:

At Miaosheo I stayed again with dear old Mrs. Wang, of whom I have written before. . . . Her husband was a real man of God. Once or twice a month he would go to Chiki to attend the services. Having over twenty miles to walk, he would start on Saturday, stay all Sunday and come back again on Monday. He would do this even in rice-planting time, when things were at their busiest. The home is one of the great old mansions in that part of the country, now worth very little, because during the Taiping Rebellion the population was so largely destroyed. When I am with Mrs. Wang, I am truly in clover, for she keeps the place very clean and cooks excellent meals. She knows what the foreigner likes and what is good for him, and just hovers over you like the dear old grandmother she is.

After the Li home with all its squabbles, it was delightful to see Mrs. Wang and her daughter-in-law together. The way the younger woman ran off to fetch a wrap, when it grew cool one evening, and threw it around the older one, spoke volumes for mutual love and respect. . . . I have happy memories of the times of family worship with them all. How they listened as we went through Psalms 22, 23, and 24, and as we studied the subject of the Lord's second coming!

Besides visiting the church members I had some good times on the street in Miaosheo, distributing tracts, selling Gospels and witnessing for the Lord. What a wonderful Gospel we have!

John was joined by Mr. E. A. Kohfield on this journey, leaving Betty and little Helen in Wuhu, and the object they had in view was twofold. They were planning a united forward movement in the evangelization of their fields, Mr. Kohfield's being the nearest mission station to Tsingteh on the south, and they were also making careful inquiries as to the Communist situation and the condition of the crops. Large numbers of soldiers had come into the district, government troops sent to protect southern Anhwei from Communist forces, dislodged from their strongholds in the neighboring province. But the presence of the regular troops aggravated the semifamine conditions and caused a great deal of unrest. Mr. Kohfield was as eager to return to the work in Tunki as John was to occupy Tsingteh, but Mr. W. J. Hanna (the China Inland Mission superintendent in Anhwei) had requested them first of all to find out on the spot whether it was reasonably safe to do so. Mr. Kohfield wrote:

We made careful inquiries all along the way to Kinghsien and while local disturbances were reported, there was not any danger, it appeared, of communist advances. From Kinghsien we went as far as Miaosheo, arriving there on October 24. Here also there were no reports of danger concerning communist activities. On October 25 we arrived at Tsingteh, the station to which Mr. and Mrs. Stam had been appointed. A short time after our arrival we went together to call on the District Magistrate, Mr. Peng. His first words to Mr. Stam were that he should not come immediately to Tsingteh. During the conversation, however, he stated that the district was perfectly quiet, and that he could safely bring his family. He also assured the Stams protection in case of danger.

Of this same interview Mr. Hanna wrote:

Mr. Stam reported to me that while there was some banditry and thieving in the Miaosheo area, owing to the drought and shortage of food, they found the district otherwise peaceful. He told me that the Magistrate's first remark was that there were small local bandits in the district, and that when he replied, "Then we had better not come down for awhile," the Magistrate agreed. Mr. Stam then said something about not wanting to risk a meeting with communists, to which Mr. Peng emphatically answered, "Oh, no, no! There is no danger of communists here. As far as that is concerned, you may come at once and bring your family. I will guarantee your safety, and if there should be any trouble you can come to my *yamen*."

Of their further investigations, Mr. Kohfield continued:

Upon arrival at Tunki on the twenty-seventh, among the first persons we met was the District Magistrate, Mr. Lo, who at once informed us that there would be no further trouble and that we could safely return. . . . The whole of the information that we gathered from these officials was to the same effect, that it would be safe for us to return to the district, and we were given much assurance of protection.

John was not only cautious in his movements, he was truly prayerful, and had now a precious wife and child to think of as well as the work. It was not lightly therefore that he came to the same conclusion as Mr. Kohfield did, that there was no sufficient reason why they should not take up their work again in southern Anhwei. That course Mr. Hanna approved, but not before he had visited the district in person.

It is certainly true today of missionary work in China, "He that observeth the wind shall not sow; and he that regardeth the clouds shall not reap." The whole vast land is passing through a period of profound transition and unrest. If we wait till all is peaceful, how shall the present suffering generation hear the gospel? We have our unalterable commission from Him who gave His life for us—Matthew 28:18-20. The words of a great military leader in this connection give us the true perspective: "Look to your marching orders! How do they read?"

It was with joy therefore that John and Betty looked forward to the next step. John wrote to his home circle:

I know you will be praying for us as we go to Tsingteh. The Lord has wonderfully answered prayer on several points. We have a cook who promises well, and the little, one-eyed woman is turning out to be a fine helper for Betty, very efficient and pleasant. She has just surprised us by bringing two pairs of the most beautifully embroidered little shoes for the baby. Wish you could see them!

Pray that the Lord may be preparing souls in Tsingteh, and that we may take every opportunity given us and may be bold for our God. Pray for Mr. Lo, as he moves up to Miaosheo. His wife is inclined to be on the fearful side. Pray that both they and we may know the truth of that word: "God hath not given us the spirit of fear; but of power, and of love, and of a sound mind." Praise God for such a Gospel as we have to make known! Keep on praying. On our trip Kohfield and I remarked, again and again, how the Lord was undertaking for us and causing all things to work out just right.

Before they left Wuhu, an incident occurred that shows much of the heart attitude of the young couple at this time. No one knew anything about it. It has only been revealed by an entry in Betty's diary, found since their promotion.

> John and I burned $37.50 (Mex.) in stamps, to make up for cheating the Chinese Government Post Office (not meaning to) by enclosing letters to the United States in home letters, with United States stamps.

It was of course much less expensive to enclose letters to be posted in the states, with American stamps, than to put the full Chinese postage on every one, and for some time the Stams did not know that this was contrary to government regulations. As soon as they realized it, however, they determined to repay the full sum by burning the equivalent in Chinese stamps. A straw shows which way the current runs, and that unknown act of reparation is eloquent of their desire and purpose to be fully right with God in every detail of life.

On the way to Tsingteh, the Stams had the joy of introducing little Helen to their friends at Süancheng.

> Well, here we are [John wrote] at our old stamping ground, and enjoying ourselves hugely. All our stuff is packed and ready to be bumped on its way to Tsingteh by wheelbarrow, some seventy English miles.
>
> Right now, we are having a short-term Bible school in Süancheng, and the Lord is blessing. I have much enjoyed some of the sessions taken by Chinese teachers. Miss Jean Yao was very good on the tabernacle; Miss Kiang too, on Hebrews.

106

As that was their last touch with fellow missionaries and Chinese Christian leaders, it is of no little interest to see the place that John and Betty had in their affections. A letter from Mrs. G. A. Birch, of Süancheng, with whom they were staying on this visit, gives just the details one could wish.

Dear Betty and John, their memories are very fragrant. We can thank God on every remembrance of them, for they were so full of the love of Christ and their lives shone with His presence. It was a privilege to have them share our home for the months they were with us.

Betty was so sweet and always happy! She had a lovely character. No wonder John fell in love with her. Our little two-year-old David took to her at once. Aunt Betty was his ideal. If she were absent, he always wanted to know where she was. All of his baby interests he confided to Aunt Betty. He knows now that his dear Aunt Betty and Uncle John are in Heaven with the Lord Jesus, and that they are very happy there. When he heard that, he wanted the Lord Jesus to come and take him to Heaven too. David is little Helen's ardent admirer.

Betty was lovely with the Chinese. Not being very strong, she did not go out a great deal, but when women and girls came to see her, they were sure of a warm welcome. They liked Betty. The girl students asked after her, long after she had left Süancheng.

John was one of the finest Christian men we have ever met. It was a privilege to have his fellowship in the work. The Chinese were especially fond of him. Everyone, young and old, Christian or heathen, liked him. The Christians thought he would become an ideal missionary, because first of all, he was full of the love of Christ, and second, he loved the Chinese so well. He was interested in their daily lives, and was ready to help whenever he could. He always made people feel that he had time for them and wanted them. John was very faithful in making the Gospel known and also in helping the Christians, whenever he could.

We were so glad to have them with us for nine days when they were on their way to Tsingteh this autumn. When they arrived, the short-term Bible school was still in session, and all the Christians from country and city were so glad to see Betty and John again. John proudly carried Helen Priscilla over to the chapel to show her off to the Chinese friends.

That Sunday when Betty and John were with us, we had a Chinese service, led by Rev. H. A. Weller, of Anking, when little Helen and our baby John were dedicated to the Lord. . . . John carried Helen, and held her until Mr. Weller took her in his arms. Then Mr. Weller gave her to Betty. She behaved perfectly and looked so sweet in her little pink bonnet. It was a beautiful service.

It was lovely to have a few days with Betty again. I enjoyed that very much. She was a sweet practical mother. I liked to see her taking care of Baby Helen. Dear, dear Betty, she was pure gold, perfectly lovely, gentle, and sweet.

Of that dedication service John himself wrote:

It was very impressive and very blessed. Both babies behaved wonderfully, our little Helen quite enjoying herself when she was awake, doing nothing. Mr. Weller prayed that she might be like Priscilla of old —a help to the church, ministering to the saints. . . . Her Chinese name, Ai-lien, means Love Link. She surely is a darling.

10

Whether by Life or by Death

A<small>FTER THAT THERE ARE</small> not many more letters. John wrote to Mr. Gibb from Tsingteh.

> We do praise the Lord for the privilege of being here. The district seems quite peaceful now, though there are rumors of rice-stealing in country places. . . . As to our work, we are praying that the Lord will help us to build wisely and truly here. We certainly do start from just about scratch.

They were living in a large old Chinese house that had been adapted for a missionary family. Their cook and woman servant were faithful friends, and when a couple of stoves had been installed they suffered less from the cold of winter. It was the end of November when they reached Tsingteh, and having but little with them in the way of belongings it did not take long to settle in. And what a joy it was to be in a home of their own, where witnesses for Christ were so much needed!

While still a girl in college, Betty had written to one of her young brothers:

> Nobody can force a single soul, Christian (so-called) or heathen, to turn to Christ. All that the followers of Jesus have to do, all they can do, is to lift up Christ

before the world, bring Him into dingy corners and dark places of the earth where He is unknown, introduce Him to strangers, talk about Him to everybody, and live so closely with and in Him that others may see that there really is such a Person as Jesus, because some human being proves it by being like Him. That is positively all the Lord asks us to do for Him, because He Himself does all the rest.

Jesus isn't dead, you see. He is still on earth and in Heaven all the time. He's perfectly able to talk with people, and He is more powerful and more perfect even than He was on earth long ago. He is still watching and working for the salvation of the whole world. Only He can't get in touch with any human being until that person asks Him in to talk with him. And no one can ask Him in, if he has never heard of Him. That is where our work comes in—to introduce strangers to Christ; only, on His side, no one is a stranger, for Jesus knows and loves everybody.

"To introduce people to Christ," and to let Him live that others cannot help seeing Jesus—that was Betty's ambition, even more than formerly. On a piece of trampled paper, in that home in Tsingteh that had been so happy, where Christ had so truly lived, the following lines were found a little later. They were signed with her girlhood name, Elisabeth A. Scott.

Open my eyes, that I may see
This one and that one needing Thee,
Hearts that are dumb, unsatisfied,
Lives that are dead, for whom Christ died.

Open my eyes in sympathy,
Clear into man's deep soul to see;
Wise with Thy wisdom to discern,
And with Thy heart of love to yearn.

Open my eyes in faith, I pray;
Give me the strength to speak today,
Someone to bring, dear Lord, to Thee:
Use me, O Lord, use even me.

And so the end drew near—utterly unexpected, and yet prepared for in God's own wonderful way. On the last day of their home life together (December 5) John was writing to friends in Paterson:

> Things are always happening otherwise than one expects. . . . The Lord help us to be quite satisfied, whatever He sends our way this day. Whether our hopes for study or work are realized or not, may He help us to be satisfied with His plan for the day, as He unfolds it to us. Talk about being a "spectacle"!¹ The Chinese has it (and rightly so from the original) that we are made to be like a theatrical play, at which others come to look. If ever you get to the foreign field you will know what that means. All that you wear and eat, all that you do and say comes in for the closest scrutiny and not a little comment. Hence the special need for prayer that God will help His missionaries to shine for Him every hour.

Some time previously John had written for the Easter magazine compiled by the students at Anking a brief meditation on a passage that was often in his mind, John 12:24-28. He dwelt on the historical connection of the words: "Except a corn of wheat fall into the ground and die, it abideth alone: but if it die, it bringeth forth much fruit," and then came to the great utterance: "Now is my soul troubled; and what shall I say? Father, save me from this hour: but for this cause came I unto this hour. Father, glorify thy name." Much comfort and strengthening had come to John himself through the implication of those words: "For this cause came I unto this hour."

111

In our own lives it is well to remember that God's supervision is so blessedly true that at any given moment we may stop, and whether we face suffering or joy, times of intense activity and responsibility or times of rest and leisure, whatever we may face we may say, "For this cause came I unto this hour." All of our social, church, and family background, all of our training, conscious and unconscious, has been to prepare us to meet the present circumstances, and to meet them to the glory of His name. This will bring us to our tasks relieved of a shrinking that would unnerve us, conscious of the fact that He who uses "a worm to thresh mountains" can use us too. "For this cause came I unto this hour. Father, glorify thy name."

So it was not unprepared that John and Betty met the sudden, unexpected attack of the Red forces that captured the city of Tsingteh on December 6. Crossing the mountains by unfrequented paths, they came in behind the government army, sixty miles to the south. With scarcely any warning, their advance guard scaled the city wall and threw open the gates. It was early morning. Betty was bathing little Helen when the first messenger came, telling them of danger. Another and another quickly followed. The district magistrate, after a short, ineffectual resistance, had fled. Chairs and coolies were obtained as quickly as possible, but before an escape could be made, firing was heard on the streets—the looting of the city had begun.

Then John and Betty knelt with their faithful servants in prayer. They were perfectly composed, and even when the Reds thundered at the door, they opened to them with quiet courtesy. While John was talking with the leaders, trying to satisfy their demands for goods and money, Betty actually served them with tea and cakes. But courtesy was as useless as resistance

112

would have been. John was bound and carried off to the communist headquarters, and before long they returned for Betty and the baby. The cook and maid pleaded to go with them, and were only deterred when the Reds would have shot them down.

"It is better that you stay here," whispered Betty. "If anything happens to us, look out for the baby."

A few hours later, John managed to write the following letter amid all the carnage and horror:

Tsingteh, An.
December 6, 1934

China Inland Mission,
     Shanghai.
Dear Brethren,

My wife, baby and myself are today in the hands of the communists, in the city of Tsingteh. Their demand is twenty thousand dollars for our release.

All our possessions and stores are in their hands, but we praise God for peace in our hearts and a meal tonight. God grant you wisdom in what you do, and us fortitude, courage, and peace of heart. He is able—and a wonderful Friend in such a time.

Things happened so quickly this A.M. They were in the city just a few hours after the ever-persistent rumors really became alarming, so that we could not prepare to leave in time. We were just too late.

The Lord bless you and guide you, and as for us, may God be glorified whether by life or by death.

In Him,
John C. Stam

[1] 1 Corinthians 4:9.

11

Spikenard Very Precious

AN ARMY OF TWO THOUSAND COMMUNISTS, soon increased to six thousand, was now in possession of the district, and the people, already suffering from semifamine conditions, had to see their meager supplies disappear as before hungry locusts. But that was a minor misery. For when the Reds abandoned Tsingteh the next morning, they left many dead behind them and carried away many captives. Their next destination was Miaosheo, the little town twelve miles across the mountains; and how John and Betty must have dreaded what that would mean for their dear friends there.

Over that familiar road John walked, a prisoner, carrying his precious little one, not yet three months old. Betty was on horseback part of the way, and they both smiled at the few people who saw them as they passed. That little Helen was there at all seems to have been the first miracle in her deliverance, for her life was to have been taken even before they left Tsingteh. Part of the torture of her parents, it is stated, was that their captors discussed before them whether or not they should kill the infant at once to save trouble. And that would have been done, but that an unexpected protest was raised by one who was looking on. Who he was or where he came from does not appear. He had been released from prison by the Communists when they sacked the town, and now dared to come forward and urge that the baby at any rate had done nothing worthy of death.

"Then it's your life for hers!" was the angry retort.

"I am willing," replied the old farmer. And it is stated that he was killed on the spot.

At any rate the little life was spared, and John and Betty had their treasure with them as they traveled wearily over the mountains to Miaosheo.

Arriving in the town, how they must have longed to go to the home of their friends, the Wangs! But terror reigned supreme. All who could had fled before the looting of the place began. Betty and John were hurried into the postmaster's shop and left there under guard, thankful to be out of sight of all that was taking place.

"Where are you going?" asked the postmaster, when he recognized the prisoners.

"We do not know where they are going," John answered simply, "but we are going to heaven."

The postmaster offered them fruit to eat. Betty took some —she had the baby to nurse —but John made the most of the opportunity for writing again to Shanghai. This note he entrusted to the postmaster to forward for him.

Miaosheo, An.
December 7, 1934

China inland Mission
Dear Brethren,

We are in the hands of the communists here, being taken from Tsingteh when they passed through yesterday. I tried to persuade them to let my wife and baby go back from Tsingteh with a letter to you, but they wouldn't let her, and so we both made the trip to Miaosheo today, my wife traveling part of the way on a horse.

They want $20,000 before they will free us, which we have told them we are sure will not be paid. Famine relief money and our personal money and effects are all in their hands.

God give you wisdom in what you do and give us grace and fortitude. He is able.

Yours in Him,
John C. Stam

Not a word of self-pity or of fear. Not a sign of faltering. He who had sent them was with them. They were strong in the quiet strength of Him who said: "For this cause came I unto this hour. Father glorify thy name."

Afraid? Of What?
To feel the spirit's glad release?
To pass from pain to perfect peace,
The strife and strain of life to cease?
Afraid—of that?

Afraid? Of What?
Afraid to see the Savior's face,
To hear His welcome, and to trace
The glory gleam from wounds of grace?
Afraid—of that?

Afraid? Of What?
A flash, a crash, a pierced heart;
Darkness, light, O Heaven's art!
A wound of His counterpart!
Afraid—of that?

Afraid? Of What?
To do by death what life could not—
Baptize with blood a stony plot,
Till souls shall blossom from the spot?
Afraid—of that?[1]

"Baptize with blood a stony plot, till souls shall blos-

117

som from the spot"—oh, how John and Betty longed, whether by life or by death, to win precious souls to Christ from South Anhwei!

Little remains to be told for, thank God, their sufferings were not prolonged. When the Communists again turned their attention to them, they were taken to a house belonging to some wealthy man who had fled. There they were put in a room in an inner courtyard, closely guarded by soldiers, and though Betty seems to have been left free to care for the baby, John was tightly bound with ropes to a post of the high, heavy bed.

How long must have seemed the hours of that winter night when he was not able to move or even change his position!

> I'm standing, Lord:
> There is a mist that blinds my sight.
> Steep jagged rocks, front, left, and right,
> Lower, dim, gigantic, in the night.
> Where is the way?

> I'm standing, Lord:
> The black rock hems me in behind.
> Above my head a moaning wind
> Chills and oppresses heart and mind.
> I am afraid!

> He answered me, and on His face
> A look ineffable of grace,
> Of perfect, understanding love,
> Which all my murmuring did remove.

> I'm standing, Lord:
> Since Thou hast spoken, Lord, I see
> Thou hast beset—these rocks are Thee!
> And, since Thy love encloses me,
> I stand and sing.

No one knows what passed between John and Betty. Those hours are sacred to Him who, for love of us, hung long hours in darkness upon a cross. Certain it is that His love, His nearness strengthened them, for Betty was able to plan with all a mother's tenderness for the infant they might have to leave behind, alone and orphaned. Could that little life survive? And if it did, what then? But had they not given her to God in that so-recent dedication service? Would He not care for His own?

Never was that little one more precious than when they looked their last on her baby sweetness, as they were summoned next morning and led out to die. Yet there was no weakening. Those who witnessed the tragedy marveled, as they testify, at the calmness with which both John and Betty faced the worst their misguided enemies could do. Theirs was the moral, spiritual triumph in that hour when the very forces of hell seemed to be let loose. Painfully bound with ropes, their hands behind them, stripped of their outer garments and John barefooted (he had given Betty his socks to wear), they passed down the street where he was known to many, while the Reds shouted their ridicule and called the people to come and see the execution.

Like their Master, they were led up a little hill outside the town. There, in a clump of pine trees, the communists harangued the unwilling onlookers, too terror-stricken to utter protest. But one man broke the ranks! The doctor of the place and a Christian expressed the feelings of many when he fell on his knees and pleaded for the life of his friends. Angrily repulsed by the Reds, he still persisted, until he was dragged away as prisoner, to suffer death when it appeared that he too was a follower of Christ.

John had turned to the leader of the band, asking mercy for that man, when he was sharply ordered to kneel—and the look of joy on his face afterward told of the unseen Presence with them as his spirit was released. Betty was seen to quiver, but only for a moment. Bound as she was, she fell on her knees beside him. A quick command, the flash of a sword, which mercifully she did not see—and they were reunited.

> Absent from the body . . . present with the Lord.
> Thanks be to God, which giveth us the victory through our Lord Jesus Christ.

Cabled home, the news brought anguish to many a stricken heart, and prayer went up day and night for the helpless little one, alone amid such dangers. From the Stam home in Paterson came the following reply to a telegram of sympathy from the mission headquarters:

> Deeply appreciate your consolation. Sacrifice seems great, but not too great for Him who gave Himself for us. Experiencing God's grace. Believe wholeheartedly Romans 8:28.

To sorrowing friends Mr. Stam wrote at the same time:

> Our dear children, John and Betty, have gone to be with the Lord. They loved Him. They served Him and now they are with Him. What could be more glorious? It is true, the manner in which they were sent out of this world was a shock to us all, but whatever of suffering they may have endured is now past, and they are both infinitely blessed with the joys of Heaven.
>
> As for those of us who have been left behind, we are reminded by a telegram from one of John's former schoolmates, "Remember, you gave John to God, not to China." Our hearts, though bowed for a little while

with sadness, answered, "Amen." It was our desire that he as well as we should serve the Lord, and if that could be better done by death than life, we would have it so. The sacrifice may seem great now, but no sacrifice is too great to make for Him who gave Himself for us.

We are earnestly praying that it will all be for God's glory and the salvation of souls. How glad we shall be if through this dreadful experience many souls shall be won for the Lord Jesus. How glad we shall be if many dear Christian young people shall be inspired to give themselves to the Lord as never before, in a life of sacrifice and service!

We are honored by having sons and daughters minister for our Lord among the heathen, but we are more signally honored that two of them have received the martyr's crown.

We are sure that our dear brother and sister, Dr. and Mrs. C. E. Scott, both join us in saying, "The Lord gave, and the Lord hath taken away; blessed be the name of the Lord."

Darkness had fallen upon the streets of Miaosheo. Behind closed doors people spoke in whispers of the tragedy of the morning. In a deserted home a little baby cried and slept alone.

All that night and on into the second day no one crossed the threshold. On the hillside where they had fallen lay the two who loved her best, silent and still. Could there have been a more helpless little life, a more hopeless situation? No one dared approach the house, for the Reds were only three miles away. They might at any time return, and their spies seemed to be everywhere. Yet as the old Bible-woman in Tsinan said through her tears: "The angels themselves took care of her!"

Hiding in the hills nearby were refugees who had fled from the Communists, hungry and homeless. And among them were the evangelist Lo and his wife who were to have come weeks before to settle in Miaosheo. Had they done so, they would have been occupying the mission premises, and would undoubtedly have been killed by the Reds or taken prisoners. Detained in unexpected ways, they only reached the town a few hours before its capture and looting. Had they been a little later, they would have met refugees on the road and would not have come at all. As it was, they had arrived and were staying the night with Mrs. Wang and her family when the trouble came.

With the first appearance of soldiers, the younger woman fled to the mountains, but evangelist Lo and Mrs. Wang's son lingered to see what was happening. The advance guard of the Reds were seeking the headman of the town, and someone pointed out those two. Wang immediately ran for his life, but Lo, not being a headman, stood his ground. He was of course taken prisoner, but Chang the medicine seller (who gave his life next day in a vain effort to save his missionary friends) was able to identify him.

"This man is a stranger here," he said. "I know him. He distributes tracts and treats diseases, as I do. He only came last night to Miaosheo."

Not realizing that "tracts" were Christian publications, the Reds gave Lo his freedom. Marveling at his deliverance, he quietly walked away, and as quickly as possible joined the refugees. For two days and two nights they suffered cold and hunger in their mountain refuge, not daring to make a fire. Happily there were wild chestnuts for food, and one man had a sickle, and cut enough grass to protect them a little, in place of bedding.

122

A rumor reached them on the second day that the Reds had a foreigner captive. "Could it be the Roman Catholic priest from Tsingteh?" Lo questioned. His own missionaries had doubtless been warned in time to make their escape. But later arrivals said that there were two foreigners brought by the Reds to Miaosheo, a husband and wife, and that they had been publicly executed. Harrowing details were given; and in great distress, Lo set out to learn more about what had transpired. It was Sunday morning, December 9. From their hiding place the refugees had seen government troops come into the valley, in pursuit of the Reds. There was random fighting that had drawn the Communists away from the town. So the Wangs returned to their home, and with them Mr. Lo's wife and child, the latter very ill from cold and exposure.

The place was strangely quiet, and even from people who were about, Lo could learn very little. No one dared speak out for fear of Communist spies, and his good friend the medicine seller could not be found. Just as he was leaving the street, however, to explore the hill, an old woman ventured to whisper there was a baby, a foreign baby, still alive. Urged to say more, she only pointed furtively in the direction of an empty house. Wondering what he should find, Lo entered it. Room after room showed traces of the bandit army. "The place was silent and aware." It seemed deserted. But—what was that? A little cry! Lo hastened to the inner chamber, and soon the baby, left alone for almost thirty hours, was in his kind arms.

He found her lying on the bed, just as her mother's hands and heart had planned. Safe in her sleeping bag with its zipper fastening, little Helen was warm and snug, and seemingly none the worse for her long fast. Taking her with him, Lo went on up the hill, for the saddest part of his task was yet before him.

The finding of his missionary friends was, as he wrote, "an unspeakable tragedy." Grief and horror almost overwhelmed him. But immediate action was necessary, for the Reds might be returning at any time. Fortunately Mrs. Lo was on hand to take charge of the baby. With the help of Mrs. Wang and her son, coffins were procured and the bodies wrapped in white cotton material, the only thing to be had in the town. Meanwhile a crowd had gathered on Eagle Hill, as Mr. Birch wrote a few days later:

> Nothing but sorrow and regret were expressed for the death of this fine young couple. Some even dared to curse the Reds for their crime. When they had done all they could, the three Christians bowed in prayer. Then straightening himself, Lo addressed the people.
>
> "You have seen," he said, "these wounded bodies, and you pity our friends for their suffering and death. But you should know that they are children of God. Their spirits are unharmed, and are at this moment in the presence of their heavenly Father. They came to China and to Miaosheo, not for themselves but for you, to tell you about the great love of God, that you might believe in the Lord Jesus and be eternally saved. You have heard their message. Remember, it is true. Their death proves it so. Do not forget what they told you — repent, and believe the Gospel."
>
> Lo tells me that many of the listeners wept. Personally, I have not seen tears in China, in response to our message. Why the change? Why the melted hearts? They had had a demonstration of the love and power of God, and the truth of the Gospel. We expect much fruit from the triumphant death and faithful testimony of these two Shining Ones.

But the urgent matter was to save little Helen; so leaving the coffins to the care of Mrs. Wang and her son, Lo hastened back to his family. And what distresses, what alarms lay before them! Their money and few possessions, left in Mrs. Wang's home, had all been stolen. Their little boy of four, their only son, was desperately ill. A journey of about a hundred miles had to be taken through mountainous country infested with bandits, to say nothing of Communist soldiers. And most serious of all, they had a little foreign baby to hide and to protect.

On foot and as secretly as possible they made their escape from Miaosheo, the children hidden in two large rice baskets, hanging from the ends of a bamboo carrying pole. They would have had no money to pay the brave man who undertook to carry the baskets had they not found the provision Betty had made that last night for her baby. Inside the sleeping bag she had tucked away a clean nightdress and some diapers, all she had been able to bring with her, and among them she had pinned two five-dollar bills. It was enough, just enough to provide for the little party, with the help of young Chinese mothers along the way, who gladly fed the orphan baby at Mrs. Lo's request.

It was no small cheer on that desperate journey when Mr. and Mrs. Lo, in spite of all their fears, saw their sick child come to himself again. After many hours of semiconsciousness he sat up and began to sing a hymn, and from that time steadily recovered.

Passing through Kinghsien, they were able to buy a tin of Lactogen. Mrs. Lo had been in the Wuhu Methodist hospital for Uenseng's birth and had learned the foreign way of caring for infants. She even had with her the feeding bottle used for her own baby and was able to put little Helen on a proper three hours' schedule for the rest of the way. Was it by chance that a woman thus equipped was at hand in that hour of need in a remote corner of inland China?

On December 14 Mr. Birch was alone in Süancheng, his wife being at Wuhu with the children. Just as lunch was served he heard sounds as of some unexpected arrival, followed by a knock at the door. A travel-stained woman came in, carrying a bundle. To his thankfulness, it was Mrs. Lo.

"This is all we have left," she said brokenly.

Fearing that her husband had been killed and that she only had escaped with her child, he took the bundle she held out to him, and uncovered the sleeping face of—little Helen Priscilla! Then Mr. Lo came in, having settled with the chair coolies, and the wonderful story was told which has given this little one the name of the "Miracle Baby."

And a miracle indeed it seemed when it was found that the infant was so well that not even her mother could have wished to see her happier or better provided for. The doctors in the Wuhu hospital pronounced her to be in perfect health, and all hearts were won by her appealing sweetness. To the grandparents in Tsinan, Mrs. Walton wrote while in charge of her:

> I am so anxious for you to see little Helen, for she is simply perfect! She is a beautiful baby, so well and strong and as good as gold. She scarcely ever cries. And she is such a dear combination of Betty and John. Her eyes are just like Betty's. She smiles most of her waking moments, and coos and talks so sweetly!

To Dr. and Mrs. Scott the coming of this little one to their loving care in Tsinan seemed like a resurrection from the dead.

> Everything about her deliverance tells of God's love and power. And we know that if He could bring a tiny, helpless infant, not three months old, through such

dangers in perfect safety, He could no less surely have
saved the lives of her precious parents had that been in
His divine plan for them.

Does the sacrifice seem wasted? Not to the two who
gave their all. Not to watching angels, who never had
the privilege of showing their love by sacrifice or suffering. What Betty felt about any offering of love to
Christ, however costly, comes out in her lines on
Mary's gift of "Spikenard Very Precious":

In Simon's house, in Bethany, the Master sat at meat:
Purity and strength and pity shone upon His wondrous
      face,
And the hearts of all were burning at His words of
      heavenly grace —
When a woman came and poured her precious oint-
      ment on His feet.

Fragrance as of eastern gardens lingered sweetly in the
      air;
And the box that held the perfume, alabaster, exquisite,
Shattered lay upon the floor, a rainbow curving in each
      bit —
As a woman, kneeling, weeping, wiped His feet upon
      her hair.

Then to disapproving murmurs the assembled guests
      gave vent:
For the world cannot endure the "wasting" of a pre-
      cious thing,
When it is a gift of utter consecration to the King —
But a woman, loving greatly, kissed His feet and found
      content.

[1]For the authorship of this poem, see page 84.

127

12

Thou Art Worthy

IT IS A TRIUMPH SONG sung in heaven. Listen! Can we catch its meaning?

Worthy is the Lamb that hath been slain to receive the power, and riches, and wisdom, and might, and honor, and glory and blessing.

It is a song of joy and praise, the Hallelujah Chorus of the universe.

And who are the singers there? Those redeemed out of "every tribe and tongue and people and nation," many of whom came from the furnace of affliction, but whose tears are forever wiped away. It is the sublimation of all earth's "songs in the night," from hearts that suffer for and with their Lord.

The Christian sings, and sings in tribulation. Prison walls heard the praises of Paul and Silas, and Peter's epistles of suffering are the pages that tell of "joy unspeakable and full of glory."

The Christian is the greatest of all paradoxes: a being who is "corrupt and yet purified, mortal and yet immortal, fallen but yet exalted far above principalities and powers, sorrowful yet always rejoicing."[1] And his sorrows become fruitful in blessing for others. So the enemy overreaches himself. Not only is he unable really to harm any child of God, but he is unable to stay the triumph of the truth, though he seeks to quench it in blood.

When Patrick Hamilton was burned in Scotland, someone dared to say to his persecutors: "If you are going to burn any more, you had better do it in a cellar, for the smoke of Hamilton's burning has opened the eyes of hundreds."

"It is always so," Spurgeon commented. "Suffering saints are living seed."

Such seed has been sown the wide world over through the experiences of John and Betty Stam and their little one, and the harvest is being reaped with wonder and thankfulness. Why did seven hundred students stand up in that great memorial service held in the Moody Bible Institute to consecrate their lives to missionary work whenever God might call them? Whence the vision that is dawning upon young people in many lands of the privilege of sacrifice and suffering in fellowship with Christ?

What has this tragedy really done?

It has opened the deep springs of faith and love in countless hearts. How they are flowing today! How they bear witness to the true, underlying oneness of the people of God! By a single mail Dr. and Mrs. Scott received letters of comfort from Australia, New Zealand, Germany, Arabia, Sweden, Hong Kong, Canada, England, and the United States. And not letters only — gifts, especially to little Helen Priscilla, came from all directions. They came from humble, unknown believers, from Chinese Christians, from presbyteries, from a bishop, from the general assembly of a great church, and from student and college faculties, notably that of Wilson, Betty's alma mater.

From the Moody Bible Institute, Dr. James M. Gray wrote to Mr. and Mrs. Stam in Paterson:

> It is needless to tell you of the high standing attained by your son and his wife in our student body, where they will be long and tenderly remembered for the witness they bore to Christ by their lives as well as their lips. . . .
>
> I trust that already in the poignancy of your grief you have had strength to lift your eyes to the glory that awaited them, as beyond the veil they met their Saviour for whom they died. No higher honor on earth could come to parents than that which is now yours, and I pray that you are walking today in the holy joy of it.

In a city of the Midwest, a Hollander came to the pastor of his church with two checks for fifty dollars each. One of them was for the China Inland Mission. He was deeply moved as he said:

"We are not rich; but we have enough. Peter Stam gave his son John. What is this in comparison?"

A fellow student of Betty's wrote with a full heart:

> I am Billie, the bugler from Indian Hill Camp. It was Betty who led me to the Lord there and gave me my first Bible. . . . Her friendship was very precious to me, and I thought you would like to hear from one at this time whom she led to the Lord. Salvation is such a precious thing that we can't help having a special love for the one who led us to Him.

There was not a dry eye in the memorial service at Wilson College. Students have written of it as the most impressive service, spiritually, that they ever attended. President Warfield got up from a sick bed of weeks to give the address. And of a similar occasion at one of the chapel services, a member of the faculty wrote:

Dr. Warfield sat in a front seat. After the sermon, trembling, he ascended the platform and in a voice broken with emotion he spoke of Betty and the baby and claimed the latter for Wilson College in the sweetest paternal fashion.[2]

We are going to watch the development of God's wonderful grace that will surely come out of all this.

A fellow worker in China wrote with vision:

We all go Home in some way! Your dear daughter and her husband have gone in a chariot of fire. . . . Now, full of vigor, their lives, their personalities, their work, their witnessing are known in every town and city of our land. A life which had the longest span of years might not have been able to do one-hundredth of the work for Christ which they had done in a day.

And another China missionary told of the reaction of some of her students:

Yesterday, seventeen young women sat round my table as I told them the story of Betty and her husband.

"Just to think," said one of them, "that little baby will one day say to us, 'My mother gave her life that you might know of Jesus.' "

It was a memorable hour.

But to come closer home; what springs of faith and love have been released in the hearts of those most bereaved! What echoes we catch in their letters of the triumph song of Heaven! To Dr. and Mrs. Scott, their daughter Helen (Mrs. Mahy) wrote:

Dearest Daddy and Mother, you don't need to hear me say how much we love you and are thinking of and praying for you in these dark days. Surely as you know your children, you know how united we are in this, every one of us, though it is hard to find words to express it. . . .

I have such a radiant picture of Betty and John standing with their palms of victory before the Throne, singing a song of pure joy because they had given everything they had to their Master, that I cannot break loose
and cry about it as people must expect. Crying seems to
be too petty for a thing that was so manifestly in God's
hands alone; but my heart is very, very sore for you.

From Davidson College, North Carolina, came the
younger brother's comfort letter:

Many people would call our loss of Betty and John a
terrible tragedy that should fill us with misery and de-
spair. But I do not see it in this way, because I am a
Christian and can see God's hand behind it all. Instead
of throwing us into despondency, it fills us with a
greater trust in God, and a greater determination to
serve Him with our lives. We do not see the meaning of
it all, now, but some day we shall understand.

In God's work the value of a life lived for Him is
measured not by length but by quality of service, and
by the fulfillment of His purposes for that life. Surely
His purposes were fulfilled in Betty and John, and are
being fulfilled: so their service was completed.

The older brother at Princeton Seminary was, as he
wrote, "badly shocked" and full of grief for his parents.
Yet he could say:

Knowing your faith, I know this thing has not got you
down. That's what it means to be Christians—that no
trial of life can be too heavy for us, for we can see the
hand of God operating in the dimness of the
shadows. . . . We have God Himself, who doeth all
things well in His infinite wisdom and goodness, as the
guardian and buttress of our hearts at this time.

I know, if your experience has been at all like mine,
that this wicked deed has jolted us powerfully out of
the spiritual lethargy into which we had slipped, and

133

that even though we thought we were giving our best, it wasn't enough and lacked the depth of consecration and the power of witness that we ought to have as God's ambassadors to men. May God release to the whole Church new power through this tragedy, and a deeper consecration and more faithful witness to the wonderful cause of Christ, for which true followers all down the ages have been ready and willing to die.[3]

And from the Congo came understanding letters from John's missionary brother, Harry Stam, who had heard the news by cablegram:

How sad and yet how glorious! How sad to think of the sin and hatred in the heart of man! And death is still an enemy. But how glorious the welcome that was theirs in Heaven, as they met their Lord and Savior face to face! It almost makes one envy them, just a little, to think of the infinite tenderness with which He must have said, "Well done . . . thou has been faithful. . . ."

We do not expect that wounds will not hurt; but we know that years ago you gave us all to the Lord, and He will in these days be speaking blessed comfort to your hearts, as He is to ours. It seems I cannot think of much save the glory of it. . . . It daily becomes more wonderful to rest in His perfect will. "Blessed is he whosoever shall not be offended in me."

In Paterson one lady said with grief: "Oh, why did they go there!"

"Because the love of Christ constrained them," Father Stam replied. "They loved the Lord and the Chinese people—that's why they went to China. We were glad to see them go, and would gladly have let them go again, because we look not at the things which are seen. They were not after money or comfort, but after souls."

"John and Betty had heavenly perspective," wrote Dr. Scott. "Given that, all other things fall into their proper proportions."

"Heavenly perspective"—thank God, many a young heart, looking forward to life's opportunity is being brought to John's and Betty's point of view. From Washington and Lee University, Virginia, one of the sons of the martyred missionary referred to in a previous chapter wrote to Mr. and Mrs. Stam:

> As my father was captured and killed by bandits three years ago in North China, I feel that I may offer you my sympathy. But what a blessed privilege is ours in having our own dear ones go the limit in service for the Master! To me, this joy has taken the place of sorrow.

And another brother, also a student at Washington and Lee and a prospective missionary, added:

> I am so glad to hear that the little girl is safe. Who knows but that some day she may serve the Lord—as I hope to, by His help—in that land where I was born and which I love.

When Dr. Glover wrote to a friend of Betty's, already a candidate for the China Inland Mission, to test her reaction to the situation in China, he was moved by her reply:

> I really believe that I have faced the possibilities and counted the cost. . . . These tragic and fearful happenings do not scare me out, but rather make me re-gird myself with the armor of the Spirit.

From Anhwei itself, Mr. Hanna writes of the attitude of John's and Betty's own colleagues, those who are left to close up the ranks and carry on the work:

> We thank God for the steadfastness of our fellow workers during those trying days. Not one hesitant or

despondent note has been heard, but all remain constant and true—"rejoicing in hope; patient in tribulation; continuing instant in prayer."

To them and all who stand for us—nay, for Him—in the high places of the field, Betty's vision of our incomparable leader must appeal:

Oh, the tongues of flame about Him were
    scarlet and hard and hot;
But the Son of man, with the eyes of God,
    loved the world and faltered not.

What has this tragedy really done?

Above all, it has set free streams of divine power and blessing. Never was there a more dreadful tragedy than that of Calvary. God's own Son went to the depths of suffering and humiliation. And then, for that very reason, God could work. "*Wherefore* God also hath highly exalted him." And more than that: it was not only power that was set free, but deeper springs of divine love. For the Lord Himself said: "*Therefore* doth my Father love me, because I lay down my life for the sheep."

Does not a great, unchanging principle lie behind the words, "Wherefore God also"? Betty caught a glimpse of it in her "Song of Sending,"[4] when she wrote:

"That man I need to move the world
Who gives Me all, to Me is all."

For sacrifice in carrying out the divine purposes of redemption sets free the great reserves of divine power and love.

We see it in the triumph song, "Worthy art thou, for thou wast slain." We see it all down the ages, in the

136

experience of those who "follow the Lamb whithersoever he goeth." We see it today in the suffering and victory of John and Betty Stam, which have set free divine forces the extent of whose working none can measure.

What share have we, each one, in this glorious forward movement of God's redeeming grace? What is there in our lives that He can recompense? What is there to call forth that deeper response of His love?

A Song of Sending

When Christ the Saviour lived on earth,
  Long, long ago, long years ago,
He bade us tell to all the world,
  "God loves you! He loves you so!"
He gave command to heal the sick
  From sin-wrought woe, all sin-wrought woe;
He said to cleanse the leper, too,
  As white as snow, yes, white as snow.

Lord Jesus, Thou are waiting still.
  We hear Thee call, so clearly call;
"Who loves Me, forth! and follow me!
  Though weak and small, so weak and small,
In God's own Spirit shall he go,
  He shall not fall, no, never fall;
That man I need to move the world,
  Who gives Me all, to Me his all."

See, all the careless multitudes
  Are passing by, now passing by.
The world is sick with sin and woe.
  All men must die, some day must die.
The time set for our Lord's return
  Is drawing nigh, draws ever nigh.
Send us in all Thy cleansing power —
  Lord, here am I! Here, Lord, am I!

[1]See Spurgeon's sermon on 1 Peter 1:6, *The Christian's Heaviness and Rejoicing.*

[2]Wilson did a unique thing in making little Helen Priscilla "The College Baby." Her higher education was thus insured, free of cost. The students also made a voluntary contribution of a hundred dollars and sent it to China for the baby's immediate expenses.

[3]In Betty's own family this has already been the case, for through her death, her sister, Mrs. Gordon Mahy, and her husband, the Dean of Witherspoon College, Kentucky, heard the call of God to China. The younger sister and her husband, Dr. and Mrs. Theodore Stevenson, worked in Canton.

[4]Written to the tune, "O, wert thou in the cauld, cauld blast."

A Call to Prayer

F FROM DR. C. E. SCOTT, of Tsinan, came an important letter calling attention to the urgent need for prayer on behalf of our suffering fellow believers in China. Speaking of the devotion of Mr. Chang Hsiu-sheng, who gave his life in a noble effort to protect John and Betty, and of the courage of evangelist Lo in rescuing little Helen Priscilla, Dr. Scott wrote:

> These events have brought a new revelation of the power of prayer to undergird weak Christians with spiritual strength in the face of personal peril. So remarkable were the courage and selflessness of Evangelist Lo and Mr. Chang that it is hard to believe that, only a few days earlier, both were rather uncertain in duty doing. Evangelist Lo was timid and fearful, and Mr. Chang was rather unwilling to witness for the true and living God. But Betty and John had, last fall, sent out prayer requests for these "little ones in Christ," and those prayers were wondrously answered in a Christlike unselfishness and fervor of spirit and magnificent daring on the part of these two men that have thrilled the world. . . . They illustrate Paul's grand aphorism: "God hath not given us the spirit of fear but of power, and of love, and of a sound mind."
>
> It is one thing to talk of Christian courage in the snug safety of our comfortable homes; it is quite another for these men and the others so nobly associated with them to count not their lives dear unto themselves, for Christ's sake.

In all this there is a message to our own hearts, in the words of Samuel: "God forbid that I should sin against the Lord, in ceasing to pray for you." Let us, by practice, reiterate our conviction of the duty and privilege of prayer for our friends in China, especially for those whom we know to be weak in the faith, for those needing heartcomfort and assurance in Christ, and for those in sickness of body, or in peril of life from evil men. Prayer makes the weak, strong; the cowardly, bold; the faithless, faithful. Real prayer actually, objectively, changes things.

Forget them not, O Christ, who stand
Thy vanguard in the distant land.

In flood, in flame, in dark, in dread,
Sustain, we pray, each lifted head.

Exalt them over every fear,
In peril come Thyself more near.

Thine is the work they strive to do,
Their foes so many, they so few.

Be with Thine own, Thy loved, who stand,
Christ's vanguard, in the storm-swept land.[1]

[1]This beautiful missionary hymn, or prayer, is by Margaret E. Sangster in Methodist Hymn Book, published in 1933.

Moody Press, a ministry of the Moody Bible Institute, is designed for education, evangelization and edification. If we may assist you in knowing more about Christ and the Christian life, please write us without obligation to: Moody Press, c/o MLM, Chicago, Illinois 60610.